G'day Cheek,

CULTURE = (VALUES + BEHAVIOR) x CONSISTENCY

The Unexpected Learning Moment:
Lessons in Leading a Thriving Culture
Through Lockdown 2020

by

Garry Ridge

with

Martha I. Finney

07-27-2022

TP

TELEMACHUS PRESS

THE UNEXPECTED LEARNING MOMENT

Cover design: Mavro Creative

Published by Telemachus Press, LLC
7652 Sawmill Road
Suite 304
Dublin, Ohio 43016
http://www.telemachuspress.com

Visit the authors' websites:
www.thelearningmoment.net
www.marthafinney.global

ISBN: 978-1-951744-78-6 (eBook)
ISBN: 978-1-951744-79-3 (Paperback)

Category: BUSINESS & ECONOMICS / Workplace Culture

Library of Congress Control Number: 2021908964

Version 2021.05.27

Purpose-driven, passionate people guided by values create amazing outcomes.

Garry Ridge

Table of Contents

Dedication i

WD-40 Company Values iii

Introduction vi

Part I: How It Started

Chapter 1. The WD-40 Company Tribes Story: How We Turned a
Great Company Into a Community of Belonging 3

Chapter 2. Where There is No Friction There is Flow:
The Four Pillars of the Fearless Tribe 21

Chapter 3. The Dumbest Guy in the Room is the Smartest CEO 37

Chapter 4. How to Build an Epic CHRO/CEO Relationship 40

Chapter 5. Are You An Accidental Soul-Sucking CEO? 47

Chapter 6. When Caring Collides With Candor 56

Part II: How It's Going

Chapter 7. 2020: Look Back in Gratitude 63

Chapter 8. Rank Your Values to Get It Right in the Right Order 76

Chapter 9. Leadership Lessons From Lockdown 2020 83

Chapter 10. Confidential to CEOs: Grateful for the
Gift of Belonging 105

Chapter 11. Nerves of Real 111

Chapter 12. Using Virtual Tools to Keep Our Culture Real 116

Chapter 13. It's Time to Think About Re-entry 120

Epilogue: The Never-Ending Learning Moment 125

About Garry Ridge 128

About Martha I. Finney 130

Dedication

EVERY CHILD WHO is lucky or wise (in my case, I can say with all confidence that I was lucky) eventually comes to understand the importance of having a collection of role models who will influence behaviors and decisions throughout life. Some of these role models are in person—such as our parents. Some introduce themselves to us via their books.

Of course, there was my father. What son doesn't ask himself, "What would Dad do?" at least once in his life? It was my father who advised me to join WD-40 Company when I was only 31 years old, with these words, "You can't go wrong with that stuff, son." And then my mum, whose most penetrating advice was delivered to me over the rim of the same china teacup I watched her sip from over decades. Her advice was mainly what *not* to do, especially having to do with putting people on pedestals. "Even the Queen sits down to pee," she would remind me.

Then, as I matured, I grew my committee of advisors to include the thought leaders whose wisdom I read in books. I never expected to actually meet them in person, you understand. I pulled their insights from their pages. It was this way that I met Ken Blanchard. I was 28 when I met him the same way millions of others did and still do—through one of his many books, probably his most successful, *The One Minute Manager*. I never expected to meet him in person either. Until I did.

I had carried his ideas with me when I relocated from Australia to the United States, still a young man. Because of his influence, I was already starting to think about how I would help WD-40 Company thrive in the global marketplace. And what kind of environment our people deserved to safely transform our culture into a tribe—a tribe that was safe, confident, mutually supportive of each other to learn, grow, and create the future we all aspired to. His words didn't tell me *what* to do. As with every gifted, generous teacher, he helped me understand *how* to think through my approach and options. And, in his case, through the lens of culture and values.

Cynics tell us never to meet our gurus in person. Nobody wants to see their feet of clay. But there came a day when Ken Blanchard walked into a University of San Diego classroom where I was a student. He had become my professor. And then he became my friend. Over the years, as our friendship deepened, and we even co-authored a book together, I never lost my appreciation for the authenticity of his kindness, his gentleness, his generosity, his servant leadership philosophy that he demonstrates through all his actions, interactions, and choices.

And it's safe to say that his influence as both my teacher and my friend positively impacted the journey that WD-40 Company traveled over the recent decades, but most essentially during 2020-2021. You will see evidence of his role in my life and leadership philosophy in all the chapters that you read in this book.

And for this reason, I dedicate *The Unexpected Learning Moment* to my friend and mentor, Ken Blanchard. Even though we have become personal friends, I must confess I still have him on a pedestal. But because he is, in fact, Ken Blanchard, I do believe that even Mum would approve.

WD-40 Company Values

We value doing the right thing.

We do the right thing in serving our tribe, our stockholders, our customers, our products, our end-users, our suppliers and even our competitors. This means looking for the right action in every context, and asking critical questions that bring out the best course or decisions relevant to the situation and the circumstances. It also means being honest in both word and deed. Being reliable, dependable and competent. And doing what's right according to the situation and the context. If we are honest and we speak and act congruently, we will be doing what is right.

We value creating positive lasting memories in all our relationships.

As a result of our interactions with our tribe and stakeholders, we all will feel better at the end of the interaction than we did when we began; we will leave with a positive memory of it. Our stockholders should be proud to say they own our stock. Our customers should consider us a part of their business success. End-users should be glad they purchased our products, telling their friends about the quality and utility of our brands. Our company name and our many brands should become known as emblems of quality, performance and value. Our tribe members should consider each other valued friends and colleagues who share work, struggles, successes, life and laughter over the years. If we successfully live these values, the result will be a higher degree of mutual trust and respect.

We value making it better than it is today.

We value continual improvement. We are a learning organization. We are responsible for our own development and helping others to learn, as well. We celebrate our successes, then move on to new heights of achievement. We solicit ideas and solutions from all, and consistently look for ways to progress. We are comfortable with self-criticism and receiving constructive feedback. We take the time to recognize others who do the same. We endeavor not to repeat mistakes. We value the development of our people in order to enhance their skills and to improve their career opportunities. There is a special moment which occurs right at the point in time where a person gains an insight or new knowledge because of a particularly positive ... or negative ... event. We are constantly on the lookout for these "learning moments," because they are the fuel for continual improvement.

We value succeeding as a tribe while excelling as individuals.

We recognize that collective success comes first. Our organization is a global company with many different locations and tribe members spread far and wide. But everything we do is geared toward the success of the entire company. And within the company are smaller groups, whether they are functional departments or teams defined by geography. The same philosophy applies in these sub-teams. We believe the individual can't "win" at the expense of, or apart from, the tribe. But individual excellence is the

means by which our organization succeeds. And "excellence" is defined as outstanding contribution to the whole. Our mantra is one world, one company, one tribe.

We value owning it and passionately acting on it.

We get our shoes dirty. We are relentless about understanding our business and our role in impacting it. We are passionate about our end users, customers and markets, and how we can positively impact them. We act in ways that maintain our traditions while positioning us powerfully for the future. We consider carefully, act boldly, and course correct as needed.

We value sustaining the WD-40 Company economy.

We realize creating and protecting economic value for our tribe and its stakeholders is a tremendous responsibility. We take seriously the fact that many families are dependent upon the actions we take. We recognize and accept this responsibility.

Introduction

YOU'VE PROBABLY HEARD this expression: The sure-fire way to make God laugh is to make plans. There is even a play called *God Said, "Ha!"* When you hear that distant chuckling, you know that maybe things aren't going to go exactly as you had laid them out. Which isn't a welcome realization for a global corporate leader. And yet we do our best with strategies, projections, objectives, and all manner of planning sessions, daily, weekly, monthly, quarterly. We at least like to have some idea of where we're going and that we're headed in the best direction of all our possibilities. People who are counting on us to be confident in our decision-making and circumstances sleep better at night.

I learned that first-hand the moment I realized that when people ask me, "How're you doing?" what they're really asking is, "How are *we* doing?" Which, if you get right down to it is just code for, "Will I be okay?"

So we know how to make God laugh. Here's the part we don't talk about: How to provoke the universe's attention. Here's how you do it. You, as a leader, put a stake in the ground and announce to anyone and everyone who is depending on you to be steadfast in your vision, "This is what I stand for. No one and nothing will move me off my position."

That is when the universe will say, "Want to bet?" And then it challenges you to a duel.

Starting in March 2020, global CEOs who, in February, were reasonably sure they knew what they were doing, were challenged to the duel of their lives. That is when the universe delivered to us the pandemic eventually known as Covid-19. And asked us all, "So, big shot, what are you doing to do now?"

In my case, and by extension, the case of WD-40 Company, our stake in the ground has always been our commitment to our values and tribal culture. These two components allowed us to make the world a better place for all our stakeholders—most essentially our customers and our people—our *tribe members*. We became celebrated for the experience of safety, optimism, acceptance, belonging, "positive lasting memories" that we were able to create throughout the world. And so, naturally, I began to write and speak about our philosophy.

And so naturally, when Covid-19 upended almost everything throughout the world like the proverbial pigeon and the chessboard, I had to answer the question, "What do we do now?" First to myself. And then to our tribe members.

The first answer was the stake in the ground that we had firmly planted into the WD-Company culture decades ago—we are a circle of safety, as Simon Sinek refers to when he talks about tribes. We will protect each other and we will use our values as the guardrails inside which we can continue to perform and flourish, come what may.

This book traces the journey of my commitment to the WD-40 Company tribe members. Both before Covid-19 and as it has unfolded over the first 16 months or so. In keeping with a trend I'm seeing on social media, it's divided into two parts: How It Started and How It's Going. This device is usually used to tell the story of romantic relationships, weight loss, raising a litter of Labradors. But in my case, it tracks the story of WD-40 Company's commitment to its values before the universe decided to test us with an epic boomerang of planet-transforming plague.

The chapters within are drawn from blog posts and documents that I wrote during these months. The How It Started portion represents my thoughts about leadership, culture, and commitment to values long before the universe said, "Let's just see about this." The How It's Going chapters were written very much in real time as 2020 unfolded and then morphed into a more promising 2021.

As I write this Introduction, we're still very much in the beginnings of 2021. We can't be entirely sure what is in store for us for the rest of the year, or, for that matter, the years to come.

But one thing is for sure. We passed the test of our commitment to our values and our people. To say that we have put the universe in its place is just asking for more trouble. But, to date, we can look at how we look at our performance, and be humbly grateful that so far so good.

As for the future, the best we can do is stand by our stake in the ground. And do our best.

The Unexpected Learning Moment:

Lessons in Leading a Thriving Culture Through Lockdown 2020

Part I:
How It Started

Chapter 1

The WD-40 Company Tribes Story:
How We Turned a Great Company into a Community of Belonging

The natural human inclination is to come together, combine our talents, seize the opportunities and attack the danger. Leadership sets the tone and the conditions.

Simon Sinek

CONSIDER FOR A moment your upcoming interviews with candidates for that opening you have in your department. What do you suppose is on their minds as they drive up to your building, greet the receptionist, sign in, wait to be escorted to your office, and then take their seat in front of you?

"Will I get the offer?" is probably the main question, followed quickly with, "Will the salary meet my needs?" Let's assume the answer is *yes* on both counts. What's top of mind for your candidates now? They are probably thinking about whether or not they will actually enjoy being in your organization: "Will I be happy here?"

Will they believe in your products? Will they be able to stand for the mission and vision of your company's long-term goals? Will they value working with and for your customers? Perhaps most importantly to their day-to-day experience with your company, will they find a community of safe, trusted colleagues with whom they can focus their full attention, contribute their best, and then go home at the end of the day to their families happy and fulfilled?

"Will I belong here?"

In other words: "Is this my new tribe?"

If you know the famous Maslow's Hierarchy of Needs, you know that the first two levels address the most fundamental physical requirements: Food, water, warmth, rest, safety, security. In the context of a person's career, those are the essential fundamentals that we can gather into the basket marked: "Will the compensation meet my needs?" From the perspective of an ordinary company, that is translated into the equation: One unit of output = one unit of paycheck. Not very inspiring, is it?

It's the third level of Maslow's Hierarchy of Needs where the true magic begins. Belonging, love, friends. This is where all the benefits of employee engagement begin. Simply put, when individuals feel supported, accepted, proud of their colleagues, safe to be themselves so they can focus on their work, rather than squander their energies on internal politics, they can invest who they are in the mission of delivering their best work.

But, historically, companies haven't given themselves the chance to intentionally create a culture that promotes those feelings of belonging. The trend toward developing emotionally healthy company cultures is slowly emerging now. And those of us who have gone ahead on this journey owe it to the workplace world to help show the way.

At WD-40 Company, we call our culture of belonging *a tribe*. I'd like to show you how we've done it.

The Origin Story

Every tribe has the story of how it began. "In the beginning ..." The origin story always involves the search for finding a place in the cosmos. The gods tell the seas where to sit, the mountains where to rise, and the sun when to set. And children learn, as they broaden their wanderings beyond their homes—which reliably supply those first two Maslow levels of needs—that, "Yes, you are welcome, you are needed, you are wanted in this new world of yours." As such, it's fitting to start WD-40 Company's tribe story with the tale of a small boy in the Sydney suburb of Five Dock in the 1960s.

That would be me, of course. Eventually I would become CEO of WD-40 Company. But in the beginning, the origin story is about a weekly bag of candy from Mrs. Peel, a lonely, elderly shut-in who looked forward to her daily chats with the neighborhood newspaper boy. It was my first real job, and my only official duties were to deliver the newspapers and collect the subscription money. But I knew instinctively that she looked forward to our friendly, daily exchange. And there, I suppose, was my first experience of discretionary effort that is inspired by emotional connection at work. Every Friday she would greet me with a bag of candy—or *lollies*, as we say in Australia. I learned from our daily and weekly routine how powerful it can be to sincerely care about someone and make an authentic connection beyond the scope of the job description. And in return, she made me feel cared about as well.

Our relationship took a mundane newspaper subscription to a new level of authentic, human connection. And for the first time that I can remember, there was someone out in the world beyond my own family who was happy to see me.

A few years later, I learned how it felt to be critically needed and trusted. Mr. Knox had the local hardware store, where I had been doing odd jobs that were suitable for a teenager. I wasn't there for more than a couple of months when Mr. Knox threw the store keys to me and said, "Here. Take care of the store. I have to be gone for a while, and I don't know when I'll be back." His father had died unexpectedly. In his grief and upset, Mr. Knox turned to the one person he could trust and handed over his entire business for safekeeping. Because he trusted me, without a second thought, he gave me the gift of boosted self-esteem and pride in my connection to Mr. Knox and his store. That translated into an intensified dedication on my part. I made sure that the store was in even better condition by the time he got back. Again, modern employee engagement experts would call that *discretionary effort*. My teenager's mind simply called it the right thing to do.

I learned through these two friendships that our work life is one critical area of our short journey in this world where we find meaning, belonging, purpose, and identity. I learned how it felt to be on the receiving end of caring, appreciation, and trust. And I could see for myself how those feelings inspired me to do even more for the people who looked forward to seeing me each day. They taught me one of my life's most valuable early lessons: That I belonged ... because I was valued ... because I cared about the people I did business with. And that because of all that, I had a place in the world.

I discovered how good it felt to be needed, in a context outside my immediate family. It inspired me to be even more valuable to the people who needed me. And those positive experiences set me on a path where each successive career choice would one day lead me to the role of being CEO of the WD-40 Company.

It's one thing to know how good it feels to be welcomed and needed. But it's quite a different matter to consider how those feelings contribute to the health of a workplace culture, and ultimately the financial success of the company. It wasn't until I moved to California in 1994 and earned my MS in Executive Leadership at the University of San Diego in 2001 that I began to form a conscious philosophy.

It was at the university that I met Ken Blanchard, who had long been synthesizing these principles into an organized study called the *Leadership Point of View*, which introduced to the world a new way of looking at leadership as an elevating influence on our people. During that class with Ken, we began an enduring relationship in which he has served as a consistent leadership mentor to me. And I, in turn, had the privilege of serving on his board of directors for 10 years.

The workplace gift to individuals as they seek the personally restorative, healing, growing benefits of showing up every day to rejoin their workplace community in the mission of achieving common goals is the gift of belonging. It's also the gift of elevating the entire corporate story to new heights of achievement as it serves all its stakeholders. And when I began to systematically apply what I experienced growing up, combined with what I was learning about workplace culture at the university, it all came together in new company accomplishments.

In very short order, I began to synthesize these new ideas that I was learning with Ken Blanchard with a growing fascination for the nature of aboriginal tribes—communities of humans gathering together with the pur-

pose of survival for today and growth into the future. In those early days of my studies, it was more fashionable to refer to groups of coworkers as *teams*. But that wasn't quite right for what I was trying to create inside WD-40 Company. *Teams* carries a connotation that is too temporary, of the moment, focused on the single task of winning at one particular thing. I was reaching for a more deeply embedded cultural reference where win, lose, or draw, we were still together and would be well into the future.

But *tribe* ticked all the boxes. *Tribes* is about *contributing* to the whole— not individually winning and losing at all costs. Any role you can think of within an indigenous tribe has a counterpart in the corporate community. Warriors. Teachers. Nurturers. Learners. Scouts. Hunters. They can all be found inside a company structure.

Equally importantly, *tribes* also spoke to me of belonging. Of course, in a corporate setting, the possibility of termination is always an option. But in a culture that is built on a tribal philosophy, dismissing employees (we call it, "sharing them with our competitors") is a last resort of such extreme circumstance that it would be as solemn a decision as it would be if a tribe were to banish one of its members.

Once employees are psychologically safe in the knowledge that they truly belong to the group, they can invest their emotional energies to the mission of their roles inside the tribe.

Can You Do This?

And so it made a lot of sense to me to study the nature of tribes around the world. I applied two questions that are commonly asked in many business strategy sessions: "What commonalities can we see here that we can ascribe to the success of our goal scenario?" And, "What is duplicable as we move forward into the future?"

In my studies I discovered seven attributes that can be found among all tribes all over the world. No matter what specific cultural details might differentiate one group from another, these seven characteristics show up in any tribal group you can name:

- Learning and Teaching
- Values
- Belonging
- Future Focus
- Specialized Skills
- Warriors
- Celebration

To answer your question, "Can I do this?" Yes, you can. Use these seven attributes as your cultural superstructure, and you will have the organized focus you need to build up from there and fill in the details with your own cultural specifics.

Learning and Teaching

When I give speeches around the world, I routinely ask my audiences if they have ever thrown a boomerang—the essential survival tool of Australian tribes from the beginning of time. No matter where I am, hands will go up. "Ah," I then say, "have you ever thrown one so that it comes back?" All hands go down, which is to be expected.

In our modernized, global society where, for most people, sustenance can be had simply by taking a quick trip to the grocery store, boomerangs are a toy, a novelty, from a far-away land. But for the original people in the land where I come from, they were the tool that guaranteed that communities would be fed.

But first, young tribe members had to learn how to use it. They had to learn to throw it accurately so that it stunned its meaty target. Or, if it failed to hit its mark, it would at least return reliably to the hunter's hand—a difficult, but indispensable, skill that the hunter had to master. This meant that someone very patient had to teach the novice hunter. And then the next one. And the next one. As one generation of hunters learned how to feed their tribes by the effective throwing of the boomerang, the teacher then had to teach those hunters how to pass that knowledge on to the next generation. And on and on, reaching far into the future, long after the original teacher had departed the tribe.

That is the tribal leader's role. We are the elders who, as teacher and astronaut Christa McAuliffe said, touch the future.

Nelson Mandela once said, "Education is the most powerful weapon which you can use to change the world." Most of us in developed countries take our education for granted. But when you consider how in some cultures people are willing to die for the right to learn how to read, and how others will control their people by forbidding them education, it's hard to ignore how crucial learning is. (The mere fact that you are reading this report is a testament to many generations of your ancestors—likely long before your own parents—who committed themselves to the principle that their children must be educated.)

And so the leader must be committed to teaching. All the time. Likewise, however, that same leader must also be dedicated to learning. Just as young tribe members had to trust that their chief knew his way around a boomerang, as a tribal leader your credibility is built up by your obvious commitment to improving your own skill sets.

Jim Kouzes, co-author of *The Leadership Challenge*, says that there are four foundational characteristics of exemplary leadership: honesty/trust-worthiness; competence/expertise; inspiring/ forward-thinking; vision for the future. The second one—competence/expertise—depends utterly on the leaders' willingness to continue their own learning path. Competence and expertise can quickly expire in today's rapid changes in technology from new discoveries. The tribe needs to see leaders constantly building their own skill sets.

Openness to learning requires a willingness—indeed a commitment—for a leader to say, "I don't know." Especially within the hearing of other tribe members. A leader can't gain competence and expertise if they shut themselves down to learning new skills, insights, and methods. This stance might create a feeling of vulnerability at first. But there is great strength in vulnerability. It sets up the opportunity for a leader to learn something new, but it also gives fellow tribe members the opportunity to teach the leader—which perpetuates the culture of learning and teaching throughout all levels of the tribe.

This is especially relevant today when the tribal elders stand to gain as much—if not more—from the knowledge of their younger tribe members as the younger stand to gain from their elders. Any leader of Millennials will say this.

One of the turning points in my own life and career was the day I got comfortable with the three most powerful words I ever learned: "I don't know." As a new CEO, I believed that I had to know everything, to be the smartest person in the room. Which is a tremendous burden for anyone to carry. But the instant the revelation finally sank in that I was actually better off *not* being the smartest one in the room, I felt set free. Free to relax in the moment, free to listen, free to absorb new information. Free, in fact, to make my own mistakes.

Which leads me to the third and final point in the Teaching and Learning attribute of the tribe: The willingness to learn, try, and make mistakes along the way. But at WD-40 Company we don't make "mistakes." We have *Learning Moments*, which we define as "positive or negative outcomes from any situation that need to be openly and freely shared to benefit all." This concept is the bedrock of our third most important value, "Make it better than it is today."

Our tribe members are safe to have Learning Moments. They are encouraged to experiment, try new things, grow from the resulting experiences, and then report back to the rest of the tribe without fear. This attitude is what helps us grow and sustain our position as an industry leader in a very competitive marketplace—not only in our industry but also in the challenge to attract and retain the very best talent the world has to offer. As a tribe we are in search of ways to expand our capabilities, and in service of that effort we acknowledge and celebrate each new discovery. Because each new discovery leads us to the future.

Even the very name of our flagship product, WD-40 Multi-Use Product™, speaks to our tribal commitment to embracing each new journey into the unknown. Our final, immensely successful, product finally performed the way we wanted it to after 40 attempts at the formula. While, in retrospect, the success of WD-40 Multi-Use Product™ has a meant-to-be feel to it, I imagine that at formula attempts 18, 29, and 34 onward, things were looking pretty bleak for our corporate ancestors.

Jules Verne once wrote: "Science is made up of mistakes, but they are mistakes which it is useful to make, because they lead little by little to the truth." While the formulation of WD-40 Multi-Use Product™ was in-arguably science, as a tribal principle, our commitment to Learning Moments is the formula that brings us closer and closer to performance excellence and tribal wisdom. Little by little.

Values

Our values are what unite us; they bring us together in a protective eco-system of our day-to-day work and decisions. Values also set us free. They are the guidelines which, once learned and embraced, release us to focus on the activities that make us successful—both as a tribe and as individuals. When clearly written, they tell us what our tribe cherishes above everything else. And in what order of importance.

A values-driven culture offers its tribe members more than just simple one-liners stating each value. Tribe members also need context so that they can see what that value looks like in action.

For instance, at WD-40 Company our number one value is, "We value doing the right thing." Because people will inevitably interpret "we value doing the right thing" differently, particularly if they are in multiple national cultures, we need to define it more fully. And so, the following paragraph expands on the core principle:

> We do the right thing in serving our tribe, our stockholders, our customers, our products, our end-users, our suppliers, and even our competitors. This means looking for the right action in every context, and asking critical questions that bring out the best course or decisions relevant to the situation and the circumstances. It also means being honest in both word and deed. Being reliable, dependable and competent. And doing what's right according to the situation and the context. If we are honest and we speak and act congruently, we will be doing what is right.

It is only after this first value is fully articulated that we further develop the values list, each one with its accompanying description:

- We value creating positive, lasting memories in all our relationships.
- We value making it better than it is today.
- We value succeeding as a tribe while excelling as individuals.
- We value owning it and passionately acting on it.
- We value sustaining the WD-40 Company economy.

All values are critical in governing the way we make our choices and decisions for the business. But each one follows the preceding for a reason— because the preceding value informs the way we live out the successive values. Even so, I have my favorites in the way they show up in our tribe members' attitude in their work. For instance, the first line of the explanation for, "We value owning it and passionately acting on it," and how it shows up every day in the way our culture is expressed this way:

> We get our shoes dirty. We are relentless about under-standing our business and our role in impacting it. We are passionate about our end users, customers and markets, and how we can positively impact them. We act in ways that maintain our traditions while positioning us powerfully for the future. We consider carefully, act boldly, and course correct as needed.

As you can see, our values make our tribal culture come alive in the clear, unambiguous way they tell us all how we are expected to behave and establish our priorities. A strong values set also diminishes what we call "churn," that waste of precious resources by repeatedly asking and answering the same set of questions, starting with "What am I supposed to do now?" In an aboriginal society, values are more than a nice-to-have. They save calories, which are crucial to survival. Living in a subsistence condition, there is nothing to be wasted on unnecessary actions or "noise" of life, such as these kinds of questions, "What am I going to do about this? What should I do about that? What will happen to me in this gray area?"

Just as these kinds of questions take up critical calories in an aboriginal society, they also spend time and money in the corporate setting. Well-articulated values eliminate fear-based second-guessing. They focus the tribe members' attention on what is the most crucial. Whatever Learning Moment might result from the choices our tribe members make at any given point, if they make their choices based on our values, they're safe.

Belonging

Naturally, this entire conversation around the tribal culture is about *belonging*. Belonging, as it shows up in the third level of Maslow's Hierarchy of Needs, and how it appears in the day-to-day life of a healthy tribe, is about creating an experience where employees can focus on building a future for their company because they aren't obsessing about their security and survival. They feel protected, supported, and safe to be authentic in both their personalities and the way they perform their work.

The workplace experience of belonging—even in an intentional commitment to a tribal culture—is vastly different from the indigenous tribes, of course. To begin with, tribe members in the indigenous context didn't have a choice. Aside from birth, newcomers generally arrived only against their will through kidnappings and intertribal violence. Leaving the tribe was equally difficult. If they were born into the tribe, there was no getting out. Even if they were abducted into the tribe, getting out was also unlikely. According to historians, these outsiders commonly chose to stay once they got the hang of things. Even when they were given the option to return to their original culture. The tribal culture was that compelling. But otherwise, in most circumstances, should they have tried to join a different tribe, they would have discovered very quickly—and unambiguously—how it felt to be unwelcome.

As a corporate tribe leader, it's imperative to remember that your tribe members are there by choice. They can leave any time. You may have chosen them, but every day they choose to remain tribe members. This is where corporate leaders make the big mistake. The assumption is that once you have put the tribal culture in place, you can turn your attention away from your tribe and focus your energies, values, and priorities elsewhere. And soon you might find yourself to be the leader of a tribe of one—yourself.

As employers, we typically continue to focus on the first two of Maslow's list of needs as organizations, which are, of course, critical. But we often stop paying attention at "belonging," once we think each new employee is properly on board. How do we create an environment where people consistently feel that they belong? Are we dedicated to the future of their development? Do we create an atmosphere where they can go to work every day and feel safe enough to focus on their work and maybe even learn something new?

A workplace culture dedicated to the ongoing commitment of belonging is not a "set-it-and-forget-it" proposition. This is where many ego-driven (instead of empathy-driven) leaders get into trouble. If they think of belonging as a cultural value at all, they look for ways to make the attribute a self-perpetuating machine. So they can go back to thinking about what they believe is really important—mainly themselves. They worry that if they make people feel like they belong too much, maybe those tribe members will take advantage of them. Or they might slack off. It's quite the opposite. If leaders actually show their people that they care about them and that they belong, those tribe members will walk over hot coals for their leaders.

Fellow tribe members—and the way they treat each other—also play a significant role in creating a sense of belonging among each other. As powerful and as empathic as the leader might be in setting the tone and expectations for a cultural environment of accountability, trust, mutual support, and openness to learning, it all goes down the drain if peers treat each other poorly.

Belonging may start with you, the tribal leader. But it can come to a screeching halt anywhere inside the organization when tribe members betray each other. Even just once.

Future Focus

One of the key responsibilities of all tribal leaders is to create an enduring organization or group that can survive over time. Leaders need a future focus or they run out of options quickly. For instance, if you were a tribal leader in an aboriginal society that lived by a lake, it would be your responsibility to foresee a future where that lake might be dried up. So even in those early years of plenty, you would still have on your mind the question, "How do we transport our tribe to a new lake so that there would always be water for us to live on?" It's that simple. Great tribes do this.

As tribal leaders we are responsible for making sure that our tribe has access to the necessary abundance on which to thrive and prepare a place for future generations. In a business setting, we are always looking at trends pointing to a variety of versions of the future. We must pay attention to the changing landscapes and architectures of the businesses around us. We must always be open to new ideas. That's where we will find the insights and innovations that will position us to thrive in an as-yet unpredicted environment.

We understand that where we are today is indeed a great place. And we're comfortable being here. But we may not be here tomorrow. We may have to move to a new place to ensure that there is an abundance of what we need to be able to take us to the next new place in the future.

In WD-40 Company, we could have been content with our iconic "blue and yellow can with the little red top, with the sticky tape on the side," and with stores stocking our products exclusively. But we continue to innovate. We continue to create new delivery systems. We continue to look at new business opportunities and trends in usage into the future. Our future focus is to ensure that we don't run out of water to sustain our growing tribe. It's that simple.

Future focus is also bearing in mind that no matter how detailed your visioning might be, many adjustments will have to be made as the reality of the future sets in. You can't do this alone. You must draw in talent—even unexpected talent with specialized skills—to help position your company to anticipate a variety of futures and be prepared to meet a new set of opportunities.

Leaders must look as far ahead as their imagination can muster. Ten years. Twenty. Why not fifty? Look ahead as far as you want your tribe to exist.

Specialized Skills

You can't do any of this alone. You must involve other people. People who are better than you in doing what they do. In any tribe there are better hunters, better fishermen, better builders, better spear makers, better fighters, better farmers. The job of the tribal leader is to know who is who, so they can be deployed exactly as they are needed, when their services are required.

It's not enough to know what is needed today; it is likely too late to get that talent identified and in place in a just-in-time scenario. Great leaders know what skills are likely to be needed around future corners, and who is most likely to be able to meet those demands. And then the planning and nurturing begin.

If, as a tribal leader, you don't have your radar tuned to discover what competencies might be needed, and how those competencies will help strengthen the tribe and the business, the tribe will start to weaken because other tribes now have the advantage. If you ignore the earliest signs of potential trends, you will be vanquished by your competitors.

As corporate leaders, we have advantages that indigenous tribes did not in that we have systems that allow us to identify the specialized talents and strengths of our current employees—whom we can then tap for further skills development. When you know where the natural strengths lie in each of your people, you can then assign further training that will enhance those strengths by layering on skills that will differentiate your tribe from your competitors.

Warriors

Business can be as fun as you want to make it. (Personally, I prefer a workplace culture where my tribe members are joyful in the work they do and who they do it with.) But let's not lose sight of the fact that it's also competition, with serious stakes involved. To be a market leader, we must have a warrior spirit. We can be happy warriors, true. But we have to be warriors all the same. We have to be warriors for the cause of the company. But also for the sake of our fellow tribe members.

In his book, *Tribe: On Homecoming and Belonging,* Sebastian Junger puts it this way: "The earliest and most basic definition of community—of tribe— would be the group of people that you both help feed and help defend." Up until this point we have focused on the "feed" aspect of the tribal experience—nurturing our people in all the elements that provide them with a sense of psychological and physical safety. And now, in the service of defending them, we need warriors—a critical category of the tribal environment.

We need a sense of *esprit de corps*, a collective understanding that all-out group effort in the service of a single mission is required. But it doesn't have to be grim and gritty. The spirit of tribal warriors can be uplifting and engaging. For instance, think of the team effort of any Southwest Airlines crew that will do what it takes to turn a plane around in record time and get it back in the air, filled with passengers who were just entertained by an utterly original safety orientation presentation.

Or that spirit can raise goose bumps, calling up the spirit of true warriors from the past. Think of the Haka tradition, now brought to the world by the inimitable All Blacks rugby team from New Zealand, at the beginning of every game. There is no ignoring the ancient Maori influence in its ferociousness. Only now, the rugby players—as well as the spectators—can best be described as happy warriors.

In the corporate setting, the culture of happy warrior infuses the workplace experience with that unmistakable sense of "whatever it takes" commitment to the mission, even head-to-head competition with another company. There's a fighting spirit, to be sure, but there is also a sense of joyfulness, of play, of loving the game.

This isn't gladiator-level competition at the Roman coliseum. There were many people in that era who had very bad days as a consequence of their engagement on the field—the winners and losers alike. The losers, naturally, had it worse. But the winners limped back to their prisons at the end of the day pretty beaten up as well. Unlike those ancient days, everyone involved in our modern business competition is likely to go home whole, with nothing bleeding, and with career still intact.

In modern day tribes, the playing field could involve another business competitor. Or maybe it was last year's metrics we're trying to beat. Or maybe how well we create positive, lasting memories for our customers. Our field is our values, and we play to the expectations our tribal culture sets for us, as individuals and as teams.

Celebration

In tribal cultures, members set time aside to mark important occasions and/or recognize star players. There is ritual of some sort, designed to call attention to the truly momentous moment. Warriors coming home victorious from a battle. Rites of passage for the youngest tribe members.

Naming ceremonies. Noting the passing of a significant season. Appreciating a critical gift of time or even nature—like the rain or a harvest.

In the corporate world, celebration is an appreciation of the people. And it requires intention. As Ken Blanchard has said, "It's a shame that most people only know that they have done a good job because no one yelled at them that day." That translates into some real numbers, which are impactful to data-driven leaders. According to a report from O.C. Tanner:

- 79% of employees who quit their jobs cite a lack of appreciation as a key reason for leaving.
- 65% of North Americans report that they weren't recognized even once in the previous year.
- The U.S. Department of Labor statistics report that the main reason people leave their employers is because they "don't feel appreciated."

According to O.C. Tanner's research, companies that have embedded recognition in their culture receive three times the return on equity than those that don't; and, likewise, three times the return on assets than those companies that don't.

Celebration is more than just a party. There might not even be a party at all. Above everything, it is the tribal leader's officially sponsored moment of appreciation—authentic, relevant, joyful, memorable, and reflecting all the tribe values in a single experience. Above all, tribal celebrations must be culture-specific, aligned with the qualities you want to encourage, and memorable.

The Tribe Feeds the CEO

The spiritual leader, Harvard professor and clinical psychologist Ram Das is beloved for reminding us, "We're all just walking each other home."

When I think of my role leading WD-40 Company, I remind myself that I may have introduced the tribe concept to my community there. But it is they—all those WD-40 Company members all over the world—who every day breathe life into the tribal vision and create a sustainable tradition that will long outlast any personal tenure I may have in this wonderful company that creates positive, lasting memories for millions.

I may be the CEO on paper, in press releases, in appearances on CNBC, before live audiences around the world, personally answerable to my Board of Directors and my stockholders. But I don't forget for a second that I work for my tribe members. Do I continue to teach them the basics of thriving in our changing environments—just as tribal elders in my home country of Australia have taught youngsters how to throw the boomerang for perhaps thousands of years? Do I lead the search for fresh opportunities and new horizons where we can grow and thrive just as tribal elders recognized the need to seek out new opportunities? Every day.

Do I learn from all my tribe members—young and tenured alike—who bring fresh thinking and innovative approaches to scenarios that they have been able to anticipate from their unique vantage point? Faithfully.

At the same time, my tribe members and I have so many leadership and development advantages that our indigenous tribal counterparts didn't have. I and WD-40 Company tribe members alike have choice. We can *choose* to be a part of this great mission and culture. Or not. As hiring managers and colleagues, we can carefully select the people we choose to invite into our tribes—an invitation that no one takes casually. And our potential new tribe members can choose to accept our offer or seek a tribe that more closely suits their values and vision for their own futures.

As the CEO, I choose to select the very best talent, intelligence, and passion for WD-40 Company tribe—sources from around the world. I owe this obligation to more than the brand reputation, the customers, and our stockholders. I owe it to the current tribe members—and I owe it to myself, for that matter—to invite only first-rate candidates to join us. Each hiring decision is a multi-decade opportunity to improve the tribe. We all stand to benefit from the hiring decisions we make.

Especially me. While I'm teaching my tribe, I'm likewise depending on them to teach me from their wealth of knowledge, innovation, and passion for our shared mission.

So when new candidates become new tribe members as they join our company, they will surely be asking themselves, "Will I be happy here?" "Will I fit in here?" "Is the WD-40 Company tribe authentic and sincere?"

As a tribe, we are dedicated to the answer, "Yes." I know this for a personal fact, because every day I am happy here. I fit in here. And I both experience and deliver the sincere and authentic WD-40 Company tribe promise.

I, too, am a tribe member.

Walk with the dreamers, the believers, the courageous, the cheerful, the planners, the doers, the successful people, with their heads in the clouds and their feet on the ground. Let their spirit ignite a fire within you to leave this world better than when you found it.

Wilfred Peterson

Chapter 2

Where There Is No Friction There Is Flow:
The Four Pillars of the Fearless Tribe

MULTIPLE LEADERSHIP STYLES and philosophies may bring any CEO the desired results of market performance, both on Main and Wall Streets. But the options get fewer and fewer as the CEO puts *sustainable* performance on the agenda. Throw in the ideal of a cultural sense of ease, passion, commitment that would permeate all the stakeholders of the company's activities throughout time and throughout the world, and you have only one leadership style option that will work:

The CEO must be completely dedicated to creating and sustaining a culture where all participants are free to focus, innovate, speak up, be themselves, make mistakes, be happy at work, and wholeheartedly align their personal purpose with the company's purpose. This is the requirement, even during those rare periods that demand a certain amount of personal sacrifice and faith in the leadership.

How does this kind of commitment to a positive culture at a macro level over time bring sustainability to the CEO's expectations for the company's success year over year, decade over decade? This commitment to a cultural consistency creates a community of interdependent and mutually supportive people. At WD-40 Company we call this community our *tribe*. Tribe members bring to their jobs, careers, relationships, and lives the following critical attributes:

- Fearlessness
- Resilience
- Trust
- Drive for ongoing learning and teaching
- Enthusiastic engagement while working, lavish celebration at the success of initiatives
- Selflessness (to a healthy, reasonable extent) in service of the community priorities and fellow tribe members
- Clarity of mission
- Dedication to purpose
- Joyful tapestry of unity and belonging that crosses oceans, spans time zones, melts national boundaries, and embraces the singular human spirit that makes up the WD-40 Company tribe.

What emerges from this culture—beyond the obviously desirable day-to-day experience of working with people we care about—is that truly enviable performance history on every key metric that drives WD-40 Company's success story. Wherever I go, anywhere in the world, I am asked, "How do you do that?"

To coin a phrase: The process is simple. But it's not easy. It requires commitment to high ideals at times when less-committed leaders might fold in pursuit of one more percentage point in profit, or when they must choose among an environmentally responsible ingredient, profit margin, or affordable price point for the consumer.

The business literature is filled with many fine stories of efforts that CEOs make to recruit their employees in the mission of creating a business success story. From the long-term, sincere efforts to the short-term gimmicky attempts, there is no shortage of ideas you can try in your own company. But from what I have found over time is that nothing will hold up in any kind of meaningful way until four fundamentals are in place.

I call them the *Four Pillars of the Fearless Tribe*. Imagine, for a moment, the sub-basement of a spectacular skyscraper. It's not so glamorous down there, to be sure. It's mostly bland concrete, specially formulated and poured to take on the weight of all that is above—all those details and amenities selected to please, inspire, communicate, transform, enlighten, and ignite the imagination of all who interact with the building and its occupants.

But you are unlikely to see any of that in the sub-basement. What you do see are massive, unadorned pillars. Considering the accumulated weight of all that they hold up, there are surprisingly few. In fact, the fewer the pillars, the better the engineering.

Such is also the case for the Four Pillars of the Fearless Tribe. As we have engineered the WD-40 Company's cultural structure over time, we found that these four pillars hold up the entire experience of what it means to do business within the company. Each pillar is critical. They are:

- Care
- Candor
- Accountability
- Responsibility

These are the essential structural supports, providing a distributed foundation under emotional weight that organizational psychologists refer to as *psychological safety* inside the workplace. In this document, I will first tell the story of WD-40 Company's success in metrics form. Then I will introduce to you the basic concepts of psychological safety as the academics are reporting on it today. And finally, I will describe our own four pillars, as we have identified them to be essential to holding up the culture that makes the WD-40 Company the joyful, successful tribe that it is today.

What If All Your Employees Loved Coming to Work Every Day?

To explore our tribal culture as the "secret sauce" of our successes, the first thing to do is define what we at WD-40 Company mean by the word "tribe." Simon Sinek talks about a "circle of safety," in which all the participants are collected and protected by a defining mutual agreement of values, practices, mission, purpose, and ways of doing things. There is an ongoing sense of belonging that is as consistent and dependable in the environment as the air we breathe. Once we are accepted into the group, we trust each other. We share knowledge freely and openly. We assume the best of each other's intentions at all times. We sacrifice for each other. We celebrate with each other. We honor our contributions as individuals without losing sight of the valuable, positive impact on the entire community. While no organization can achieve this state constantly or without being tested, our objective is to work toward achieving this condition at least 95% of the time.

You may recall from the previous chapter that author Sebastian Junger defines *tribe* as "the group of people that you both help feed and help defend."

Taking the effort to define and create a tribe in your company has obvious significant and unmistakable rewards. Dave Logan, John King, and Halee Fischer-Wright specify them beautifully in their book, *Tribal Leadership: Leveraging Natural Groups to Build a Thriving Organization*:

- People collaborate and work toward a noble cause, propelled from their values.
- Fear and stress go down as the "interpersonal friction" of working together decreases.
- The entire tribe shifts from resisting leadership to seeking it out.
- People seek employment in the company and stay, taking the company a long way toward winning the war for talent.
- People's engagement in work increases, and they go from "quit on the job but still on the payroll" to fully participating.
- Organizational learning becomes effortless, with the tribe actively teaching its members the latest thinking and practices.
- People's overall health statistics improve. Injury rates and sick days go down.
- Setting and implementing a successful competitive strategy becomes stunningly easy as people's aspirations, knowledge of the market, and creativity are unlocked and shared.
- People report feeling more alive and having more fun.

How has our commitment to a tribal culture manifested itself in the experience of working at WD-40 Company and our market performance?

That story is best told by the results of our 2018 Employee Engagement Index. Below are just some of the 26 queries that we have identified as key to our performance both in the marketplace globally and our own noble cause of making sure we are providing a workplace culture where our employees feel safe, supported, appreciated, inspired, innovative, curious, and optimistic. About 94% of global employees completed this survey, in seven languages:

"I am clear on the company's goals."	98.0%
"I am excited about WD-40 Company's future direction."	93.9%
"WD-40 Company encourages employees to continually improve in their job, to make it better than it is today."	93.8%
"I understand how my job contributes to achieving WD-40 Company's goals."	97.9%
"I kow what results are expected of me."	95.3%
"I feel my opinions and values are a good fit with the WD-40 Company culture."	97.5%

And, my personal favorite:

"I love to tell people that I work for WD-40 Company."	98.3%

All these answers are experience-based. The way our tribe members experience their time at WD-40 Company shapes their perceptions of the company, and whether they feel it is a good place for them to invest their time, talents, and passion. Providing those experiences is, to all of us at WD-40 Company, a sacred responsibility for multiple reasons. We recognize that people spend the majority of their waking hours at work. So why shouldn't they feel fully fulfilled and supported by people they know, like, trust, and respect? Don't we all deserve that daily expectation as part of our natural inheritance as humans in this world? And they bring those positive feelings home to their families at the end of the day. So we know that our tribe members' positive feelings about the work they do contribute to the optimism that their family members carry with them into their own futures.

How does this tribal engagement manifest in company performance? There is abundant literature showing the linkage between high engagement scores and company performance across companies and industries. So I'll just focus on what we're experiencing at WD-40 Company:

Over the past 20 years that we have committed to these foundations, our sales have quadrupled. Our market cap has increased from $250 million to nearly $2.5 billion. And during these last two decades, our annual compounded growth rate of total shareholder return is 15%.

The proof of the pudding, as they say, is in the eating. Those numbers represent a whole lot of product. But our second most important value is, "We create positive lasting memories in all of our relationships." Engagement, and thus personal investment in the organization, stems from positive experiences within the tribe, which yields the applause of financial performance.

Psychological Safety—A Brief Introduction

In this dynamic environment, successful organizations need to be managed as complex adaptive systems rather than as intricate controlled machines.

Amy C. Edmondson,
*Teaming: How Organizations Learn,
Innovate, and Compete in the Knowledge Economy*

It's been almost a century since productivity experts turned their focus on how companies can optimize production by improving the human aspect of the organizational systems. In the earliest decades, their attention was on how humans and machines could interact better, making incremental improvements—with humans standing in the service of the machines. Then, predictably, as the Knowledge Economy took predominance over the manufacturing sector, the focus was turned to how individual employees could perform better as separate functional entities—their workstations being primarily between their ears—generating each company's competitive edge through innovative, original thinking.

Consequently, over time, organizational psychologists and corporate leaders are coming to fully realize the critical role that mental health plays in a company's performance. As the Knowledge Economy evolves, we leaders are beginning to acknowledge—even, for some of us, embrace—our roles in creating a cultural experience where our people are free to contribute their best because they feel safe. As Maslow's Hierarchy of Needs has proven, without a sense of safety (survival, family preservation), it's impossible to think long term and to stay engaged. After those basic, hygienic needs are met, people then need to feel that they belong to a welcoming, non-judging tribe, where they can count on the support of others. Then they can focus on their performance, secure in the knowledge that their community of colleagues—their tribe—wish them the very best. And the feeling is reciprocal.

This is called *psychological safety*, an expression first introduced by the organizational culture pioneer Edgar Schein. Amy Edmondson, the Novartis Professor of Leadership at Harvard Business School, has subsequently developed this concept to encompass the entire team experience. Edmondson's research encourages a shift in focus from production (which she calls "organizing to execute") to a "new way of working that supports collaboration, innovation, and organizational learning."

"Learning in today's organizations involves what's called *reciprocal interdependence*, where back-and-forth communications are essential to getting the work done," Edmondson writes in *Teaming*, outlining workplace conditions where a psychologically safe culture is essential:

- When the work requires people to juggle multiple objectives with minimal oversight.
- When people must be able to shift from one situation to another while maintaining high levels of communication and tight coordination.
- When it is helpful to integrate perspectives from different disciplines.
- When collaborating across dispersed locations.
- When pre-planned coordination is impossible or unrealistic due to the changing nature of the work.
- When complex information must be processed, synthesized, and put to good use quickly.

What culture in today's global business environment does *not* have any of the elements that require team members to work together freely, generously, and fearlessly? And yet, there are so many opportunities inside every business, within every business day, where the best of intentions, the best of ideas never emerge because of a misunderstanding or perceived betrayed trust.

Edmondson adds, "The knowledge-based economy only works well when it restores workers on all levels to self-respecting, self-determining adulthood."

For this to be effective, they need to feel safe—not only physically safe but emotionally secure to focus on their work and bring new ideas to the table without fear of retribution. We at WD-40 Company celebrate the *Learning Moment*. As we have already discussed in Chapter 1, the Learning Moment is an experience with a positive or negative result, which is to be freely shared so that all can learn from the experience. It is not to be punished. Edmondson calls leaders' attention to the need for companies to emphasize their value on learning without reprisal as a key component to the psychologically safe culture. She writes:

> This calls for workers who know how to experiment, how to think on their feet, how to work in the absence of rules, and how to adapt quickly. Knowledge, changing quickly within disciplines, becomes even messier and more uncertain when integrated across disciplines ... to get things done in the new workplace. Creating an appropriate environment for teaming and learning requires different management skills and expectations from those required in a repetitive task environment ... today's managers need employees to be problem solvers and experimenters, not mere conformers.

To cultivate a culture of these confident, independently motivated, interdependent team members, leaders are increasingly recognizing the need for their entire community of talent to be integrated by a common set of values and expectations. When those are in place, people are free to focus, create, and bring your company to the fore in its competitiveness, and in its ability to attract and retain the very best talent to continue your march toward your desired future.

At WD-40 Company, this culture starts with our Four Pillars of the Fearless Tribe.

The Four Pillars Explained

Knowledge is only rumor until it lives in the bones.

Asaro tribe in Papua New Guinea,
as quoted by Brene Brown, *Dare to Lead*

The success stories of other companies are especially interesting when they carry indicators of how we can transform their examples into actionable insights to apply to our own organizations. It's one thing to know the success metrics of highly admired companies such as WD-40, but the real value is understanding the ways you can duplicate WD-40 Company's approach to the extent that's appropriate to your business.

Your culture is different, as it should be. So copying WD-40 Company's example in all its details—as you might a cookbook recipe—could set you up for failure. However, the foundational pillars that I introduced above are duplicable anywhere. No matter your industry, business, market, demographics, geographic location, these four pillars will support your own culture where your people will be proud to go to work every day. Install these four pillars, and you will have the foundational support you need to create the business that all your stakeholders will be proud to be associated with.

Care

Life is short. Do whatever you can to help people—not for status, but because the 95-year-old you will be proud if you did help people and disappointed if you didn't.

Marshall Goldsmith

Imagine the company environment where you and your people go to work every day, as a tribe you make a contribution for something bigger than yourself, you learn something new, you feel safe, and you go home happy. That's what a *caring organization* is.

As I've witnessed the concept of Care come alive at WD-40 Company, I see our commitment to creating that caring organization flip all the levers that make life inside a healthy community a good, rewarding, fulfilling place to be. The caring culture is an environment where people are given the latitude to apply the principles of basic human kindness, gratitude for all that we have, the pursuit of justice, trust, transparency in our relationships throughout the organization, and the safe experience of honest conversation (which we will explore further in the next pillar—which is Candor).

Let's first explore what the caring organization is not: It's not Friday night gatherings where we all sing *Kumbaya*. It's not about making decisions that have the least amount of negative impact on individual self-interests in the short-term. The caring organization is not a hug, a flower, or a brownie to soothe hurt feelings. The caring organization is not about creating a narrative where the CEO feels good about having the reputation for being a caring leader, at the expense of longer-term objectives.

When I consider the fundamental elements of the caring organization, along with its most basic promise, the word *trust* comes to mind. It is the ultimate value proposition of the caring organization. To break this concept down in actionable components, we draw from Cynthia Olmstead's Trust Model, as described in *Trust Works!*, the book she wrote with Ken Blanchard and Martha Lawrence. It follows the simple ABCD format:

A—Are you *able*? Are you competent?

B—Are you *believable*? Do your actions reflect your words?

C—Are you *connected*? Do you take time to be with people in a meaningful, emotionally authentic way?

D—Are you *dependable*? Do you do what you say you're going to do? Can people rely on you?

Trust is the fundamental experience of the caring community. When you have trust, you have a tribe who will trust that you have their best interests always at heart. They will follow you into high-risk, long-term territory where great business outcomes will be found.

Candor

The void created by the failure to communicate is soon filled with poison, drivel, and misrepresentation.

C. Northcote Parkinson

The second element in Olmstead's Trust Model is B for *believable*. A culture where everyone is believable (not just the leaders) is one where everyone feels safe to speak their truth as they know it. This doesn't automatically presume that everyone will agree with each version of the stated truth. But without a culture of safety where everyone can be counted on to express themselves, the entire community will forfeit the enriching benefit of all points of view.

And, as Parkinson famously noted, the result of restrained truth is a toxic stew of half-truths, misunderstandings, critical decisions made based on only partial information, fractured relationships, stifled passions, and, before long, the regrettable departure of your most cherished talent.

This pillar of Candor shows up in actual behaviors: No lying, no faking, no hiding. Period. How this shows up to the leaders: They must always be prepared to be open and receptive to unpleasant information. How this shows up to the tribe as a whole: Each tribe member feels safe to take the risk of speaking the truth. In fact, when this pillar is installed correctly, on a cultural level, each tribe member feels more at risk for *not* speaking up.

The safety is in the communication. This is the open avenue to delivering the best self that every tribe member has. Truth, told respectfully and with positive intent, creates safety.

Most people don't consider themselves to be liars. But it's safe to say that many people will fake and/or hide when they feel they must protect their best self-interests. They fear reprisal.

Faking is simply not being true to yourself and your values. We've all heard, "Fake it until you make it." People think, "I'm just going to fake this because I'm afraid that people will see that I don't know something everyone else seems to know [for the record, they could be faking as well]." Or, "People will think less of me when they realize that I'm the only one in the room who has a completely different perspective on this matter."

Hiding occurs when there is something they don't disclose because there is fear of failure; fear of some sort of negative reaction, either from the tribe or tribe leaders; or fear of being caught in having done the wrong thing—or the right thing wrong.

In the psychologically safe workplace, we all hold dear the principle that when we behave in good faith and with good intentions, there is nothing we could do that would cause us to hide. And the spirit of the learning moment, which is such a crucial component of the psychologically safe workplace, is being true to ourselves and sharing our error with our tribe members. When we are, we are bringing additional wisdom and knowledge to the group as a whole. If we hide our mistakes, we deprive our entire team of essential learning.

As we have discussed above, the essential value of the psychologically safe workplace is the promotion of flow by the absence of friction. A workplace culture devoid of trust is an experience filled with friction. Candor removes that lack of clarity, deletes the confusion, smooths the surfaces of engagement of the rough splintery texture of emotional sticking points. And candor sets the stage for clear exchange of ideas. This is the value that promotes a high-performing workplace culture.

This isn't to say that candor-based conversations are easy. Some can be tough to initiate, some even tougher to be on the receiving end. Candor is not permission to be brutal, in the name of being honest. Candor must be accompanied by caring. All tribe members—especially leaders—should take extra care to fill the emotional bank accounts of their colleagues with positivity and supportive relationship interactions. This way, when the time comes for a conversation that requires uncomfortable candor, the trust is already there. Even the toughest conversation will result in strengthened trust that will prevail over the momentary discomfort of disclosure and discussion.

Accountability

Accountability is hard. Blame is easy. One builds trust. The other destroys it.

Simon Sinek

It seems that in these modern times, *accountability* is seen as a negative thing—an occasion to punish someone should that person fall short of the agreed upon standard or goal. That person is on the hot seat, and now must *account* for their disappointing performance.

At WD-40 Company, we have a different relationship with the word *accountability*. We see it as a two-way street in which leaders and their direct reports equally hold ownership of the way we perform our duties and what outcomes our efforts lead to. For this reason, for example, we tell our leaders that their job is to make sure their direct reports have everything they need to succeed in their jobs. And all our tribe members hold ownership of making sure they have what they need to succeed and lead the company to its fulfilled objectives.

Accountability, as a pillar, is a mutual discipline. But it's not the occasion to be disciplined. The disciplined commitment to results itself is, in practice, a freedom of sorts. When the company is committed to promoting accountability in its tribe, the individuals who demonstrate accountability also hold permission to do whatever is necessary to meet that accountability.

WD-40 Company's Maniac Pledge is an example of this philosophy in action. Years ago, a direct report spent a great deal of time explaining to me why a goal was not accomplished within the agreed-upon time. The blame was placed on a lack of critical information required to take the necessary action. After hearing the tribe member out, I observed the simple truth out loud, "In the same amount of time it took you to explain to me why this commitment didn't happen, you could have acquired the information you needed to get the job done."

And at that moment the Maniac Pledge was born, named after Aussie golfer Greg Norman, who was known for his maniac spirit. It reads this way:

I am responsible for taking action, asking questions, getting answers, and making decisions. I won't wait for someone to tell me. If I need to know, I'm responsible for asking. I have no right to be offended that I didn't "get this sooner." If I'm doing something others should know about, I'm responsible for telling them.

This spells freedom—the freedom that our tribe members feel is necessary to get their job done and meet their obligations to their own direct reports, as well as to their direct supervisors. In our tribe, we don't have the victim's attitude; there are many reasons and no excuses. We face the facts, learn, and move to improve.

To us at WD-40 Company, accountability is manifested by the commitment that each tribe member holds in carrying through with their commitments. It is an understanding and expectation culturally that each one of us will own the desired outcome and all the steps required to achieve that outcome. For both ourselves and for the people throughout the organization chart who depend on us to help them be successful as well.

Accountability is achievement. But it's also learning that we are responsible for sharing with the rest of the tribe. And the community celebration when that outcome is realized.

It's fashionable to talk about "accountability partners" today. These are people we meet at the gym, on volunteer teams, or in work groups who we must rely upon on regularly for mutual support in accomplishing our goals. But, really, our first accountability partner is the face in the mirror. Are we, as individuals, at peace with our actions and choices? If we have a face-to-face conversation (with our own faces) about how well we honor integrity to ourselves, how will we hold up in the investigation? As we say at WD-40 Company, when things go right, look out the window to find all the other people who contributed. When something goes awry, look in the mirror first.

We are each our own supervisors. And we are each our own direct reports. Are we giving ourselves what we need to make sure we succeed and that we help our company succeed?

Responsibility

Too many leaders act as if the sheep ... their people ... are there for the benefit of the shepherd, not that the shepherd has responsibility for the sheep.

Ken Blanchard

Let's revisit the Maniac Pledge one more time. You probably have noticed that each item of the Pledge is driven by the words, "I am responsible for ..." *Responsible* appears three times in the Maniac Pledge. In Accountability we speak of the outcome. In Responsibility, we speak of the *relationship* each tribe member has to the ideal that generates the outcome.

Simply put, Responsibility is a turbo-charged version of Accountability. As a tribe, now that we know what we're accountable for, it's our responsibility to make sure those desirable outcomes are actually realized. We each take personal ownership of the outcomes, and it's up to each of us to do whatever it takes to make it happen. Consequences (rewards and negative feedback in its variety of forms) are attached to the Responsibility pillar.

Responsibility is each tribe member's personal relationship to their role in realizing the ideal outcome. It demands that each tribe member respond with the answer "me," when the world poses the question, "Who is there to act?"

When it comes to psychological safety inside the workplace, when each tribe member is confident that everyone else shares responsibility in the company's success, the entire community feels safe to invest their hearts, minds, talents, efforts, risks in realizing the company vision that everyone agreed to. Everyone has their part and role. And everyone performs exactly as expected, because everyone shares the responsibility of a successful outcome.

I'm reminded of a strategy in rugby called the *blind pass*. In American football, even non-fans know how marvelous it is to watch as a quarterback throws a long pass into seemingly empty air—but with every expectation that a team member is on his way and will be positioned in the right place to receive the ball when it ends its flight and drops into his hands. You don't have to be an expert football fan to be impressed by the skill, strength, accuracy and teamwork of that play.

Well, in Australian rugby, that pass is basically performed backward—hence the name *blind pass*. The quarterback is running, but throws the ball backward, without being able to see whether there is going to be a team member likely to receive the ball. That is responsibility in action because the quarterback is psychologically safe in trusting that the pass will be completed and the objective of the play will be accomplished. There will be no wasted time, motion, effort, faith, trust, or ambition because everyone holds the assumption that the ideal of responsibility is equally shared amongst them all.

Now You Have a Foundation

These four pillars are your foundation, upon which you can build strong and enduringly positive relationships among people who rely on your leadership. If you are the CEO, you have the highest likelihood of being able to spread these pillars around the organization. If you are not the CEO, you can still influence other leaders by your example. People will want to work for you. When you have openings, internal candidates will flock to apply. Your group will meet and exceed objectives more often. Your employees will be coveted by other departments. You'll have opportunities for personal growth daily, because you will be investing in your own growth by working diligently to build and preserve the pillars of a fearless tribe!

Chapter 3
The Dumbest Guy in the Room is the Smartest CEO

IT'S OFTEN SAID that the best place to make powerful contacts and to learn valuable things is in the First Class cabin of a long-haul flight—ideally across at least one or two oceans. But I'm here to tell you that ground transportation can be even better. The ride may be shorter, but it's certainly cheaper.

I was in India traveling from the airport to the hotel with one of my senior leaders when, as luck would have it, we sat next to a guy who was a supply chain expert. Not only that, but he was in the mood to talk. A lot. And, again, as luck would have it, we needed the latest thinking in this area. Thousands of dollars of free consulting, right there.

All we had to do was keep our mouths shut. Which isn't easy. There's a ridiculous part inside all of us that is driven to clue the world in on how much we know. When we override that drive to hear ourselves talk, we give ourselves the chance to hear other people talk. And then we stand to learn something.

You'll see at the bottom of my emails the motto *ancora imparo*, which means "I'm still learning." Widely misattributed to Michelangelo (ironically, we're still learning who originally said it), it's the most essential thing I can tell people about myself, especially in my role as a CEO. By being the first in the room to say, "I don't know," I'm giving others the chance to fill the void with game-changing information. Or even to admit that they don't know either, which is also critical for a leader to know.

This a-ha came to me when I first arrived in the United States from Australia in the early 1990s. I was sitting in a meeting, and it dawned on me that I was having trouble absorbing and understanding the subject at hand. I realized that I was just about to walk out of the room at meeting's end no more informed or better equipped to do my work than I had been when I walked into the room. I had better speak up soon and come clean with my not knowing.

About 20 minutes into the presentation, I raised my hand and said, "I'm sorry, I'm not long in this country, and I have no idea what you're talking about." I had naturally assumed it was me. But as it turned out no one else knew either. But no one else was brave enough to admit it. You could hear the sighs of relief.

Simon Sinek, the author of *Start With Why*, recalls a similar experience. And he says, "The risk you run is that sometimes you get humiliated. But not always. Sometimes you will get people who will say, 'Oh my gosh, me too.' But you worry that you are the idiot. If you let that stop you, you won't get the great answers."

What kinds of answers might you get if you ask the questions and let others do the talking?

You learn what the experts know. As with our loquacious friend in India, people feel good when they can hold the floor on the things they know best. We all tend to get expansive when we have a rapt audience. So let's let the experts expand; and expand our knowledge in the process.

You learn what your tribe members know ... and don't know. Let's say you're in a meeting with your tribe. Multiple levels are present. Throw out a question and sit back to watch what happens next. Likely your immediate direct reports will jump in and answer your question. You're their boss; they want to impress you. Your wise direct reports, however, will also sit back, stay quiet, and watch to see how *their* direct reports will answer the question.

Almost everyone who achieves a senior leadership role thinks they're supposed to have all the answers. But they have to remember that their job is now to lead *others* into developing and knowing the answers. If they are going to be true leaders, they have to model your behavior, and stay quiet to let others share what they know.

This means that, as with every other behavior in your organization's culture, being the dumbest person in the room starts with you.

Chapter 4
How to Build an Epic
CHRO/CEO Relationship

FOR DECADES NOW, new generations of young HR professionals eventually succumb to the temptations of their ambitions. They just can't help themselves. And so they ask The Question. "What does it take to get a seat at the table?" The generations of senior HR leaders' eye-rolls are equally predictable. The earnest and legitimate question doesn't get sufficiently answered. And the senior HR leaders are reminded of all those decades they circled around to the same needy inquiry. Again and again.

The problem with that question is this: It ignores the fact that when you're in HR, at no matter what level, you already have a seat at the table. You've already got the power. You've got the influence. What are you waiting for? Just use it. You can make a positive difference for your company wherever you are.

This question of how to get the proverbial seat at the leadership table also focuses on the self-interest of the HR newcomer, which is another invitation for an eye-roll.

Self-interest is not a powerful attribute. Desire to serve is.

That is the energy that moves you through your career so that eventually you will be partnering with someone like me, a corporate CEO who really needs what you have. And who really appreciates who you are and what you do.

It's not about the HR leader getting invited to a table of decision-making. It's about what I call *the epic CHRO/CEO relationship*. Buried deep inside the "seat at the table" question, even in the HR professional's earliest days, is the acorn of this ultimate oak-like dream—how do you line yourself up for the ultimate chance to influence powerfully and globally, to gain the trust of the most powerful individual (and C-suite team) in the room, to drive a company successfully toward its business goals, while serving hundreds, even thousands, of individuals who are looking to you for financial and career reliability? That's really not a bad gig at all. How can anyone be blamed for wanting to take the right steps as early as possible that will steer them toward that opportunity one day?

So let's talk about this epic CHRO/CEO relationship, and what makes it more compelling than the seat-at-table conversation. It's about shared vision. It's about shared creative problem-solving. It's about an intimate, trusted partnership that is unlike any other relationship either of you can count on in the organization—maybe even in life. It's about exuberantly sharing the thrilling ride of making something truly extraordinary that will change the lives of all the company's stakeholders. It's about high-stakes adventure, drama, and more than a little bit of absolute, flat-out, fun.

At least it can be, when the chemistry is right and the vision is shared.

When the relationship is epic, the stories and successes that result from this partnership will be legendary, critical reference points for inspiration.

The shared history will provide reminders for your company's leadership long after the two of you have left the building.

So it's not a seat at the table that you want. What you want is a dynamic relationship with a CEO like me: A leader who deeply respects the HR role in creating a workplace culture that animates shared purpose and vision. You need someone who appreciates you, who values the expertise and creativity you bring to the leadership conversation, who will respond to your ideas and say, "That's fabulous! Let's make it happen!"

Here's how to build that epic relationship.

We foster a shared belief that our work together is all about the people. Commitment to creating an environment based on servant leadership requires mutual agreement that our personal interests and priorities take a seat way in the back. CEOs and CHROs are often at different stages of their careers. And it's not uncommon that their personal agendas aren't quite in alignment.

The CEO, for instance, may be about ego gratification. The CHRO may be about ambition and continuing the upward career climb. Unless there is explicit commitment that their shared work is *about everybody else,* the culture of servant leadership is sacrificed. "It's all about the people," is an idea both leaders should agree on equally. And every conversation starts from that single, shared point of view. This is a bedrock value of leadership in our company, supporting our organizational values, and supported by them. The CEO and the CHRO must have identical values of leadership and organizational evolution.

You don't give me what I ask for; you help me create what I envision. HR professionals hear this piece of advice: *Don't be a minion.* And that's good advice, but it focuses primarily on the message: *Don't be an order taker.* If the CEO wants a mere order taker, the CHRO role would be eliminated entirely, and the HR function would be shoved deep into the organization at least three levels down. That approach to HR doesn't help anyone. What the CEO really wants is a collaborative, creative partner in getting the desired result. You are better positioned to know how to do that than the CEO is.

When CEOs get an idea, they commonly leap straight into deciding what action would best manifest that idea. What comes out of our mouths is the request for the action, rather than an invitation to brainstorm the multiple avenues to achieving the desired result. Remember you are the HR expert, not the CEO. You are in the best position to know what options there might be out there. Slow the CEO down and dig into inquiry as to what exactly the best result looks like.

This is where you can save the company's time, money or even its very culture.

We share a respect for both tough-minded and tender-hearted approaches to challenging business decisions. The servant leadership philosophy requires both mindsets. In the typical scenario, the CEO might come to the table with the tough-minded position, fully anticipating the CHRO to deliver the tender-hearted perspective. Adopting these predictable extremes of perspective all the time will get you and your CEO nowhere. You'll just butt heads, and eventually one of you will get sick of it, and seek a new partnership elsewhere. But acknowledging that there's value in both positions will open a space between you that is conducive to free and respectful dialogue where innovative business solutions can emerge.

You have a broad understanding about our business and its industry. Take every opportunity to be exposed to all aspects of the business. Go on sales calls. Learn supply chain management. Study the special legal ramifications of doing business in your targeted countries. What are the environmental concerns associated with our new strategy? Take the helm of an entire piece of the business when you get the chance to. Nothing prepares an HR leader for contributing to strategy better than knowing about business in general, and the one they're in specifically.

In other words, never give your peers the opportunity to say to you, "What do you know? You're just HR." They know the answer because they have invested time in helping you understand the nuances of their piece of the business. And because of that time you have spent with them, you have developed relationships with everyone on the team. They know you're committed to excellence and that you are an equal player in the forward progress of the company.

You know where the holes are, and you have solutions for filling them. Your peers at the table aren't paid to anticipate the people issues associated with their plans and strategies. You are. As we're generating great ideas for breakthroughs, innovations, and new product roll-outs, we're counting on you to know where the talent and competency gaps are, both near-term and into the far future. What does our people strategy look like five to ten years out? And does it serve the scenario we're revising on the fly in the course of a single meeting? We don't know. We're asking you. You're in charge of making sure we have the strategies for acquiring the talent we need to meet the future head on.

People, talent, competency gaps—they are natural byproducts of strategy shifts and changes. Good succession planning, for example, is really about rigorous bench-building well in advance of the need. When you help leaders do that, succession takes care of itself. But we are counting on you to be the one to get that momentum in motion.

We have a shared dedication to continuous learning. My personal motto is *ancora imparo.* Translation: "I am always learning." Michelangelo is credited for having said it when he was 87, long after most men of his era had stopped breathing altogether, never mind their commitment to learning.

It's been fashionable for several decades now to trumpet the value of a learning organization. Seems simple enough when you're talking about creating an environment where the entire employee population is expected to keep up their skills and expand their horizons. But it also means that the two of you together must constantly remind each other that you have committed to open-minded, continual personal growth. In the course of busy days, back-to-back meetings, and high-stakes strategic thinking, slowing down to learn, listen, and perhaps reconsider is an easy thing to put off.

I never lose sight of the fact that in any given assembly of my WD-40 Company tribe members I am likely to be the one who knows the least. In fact, I felt an immense, personal relief when I finally learned to love the three words, "I don't know." And so I listen with every intention of not only being informed but also influenced.

In a profession that changes as rapidly as the HR function, what can be better than to have an epic working relationship with my people partner who is equally passionate about learning? It is a never-ending adventure into new frontiers of knowledge, insights, understandings and the discoveries of fresh possibilities.

We share a mutual respect where hard conversations can be had in a safe setting. In an epic CHRO/CEO relationship, there is no fear. The CHRO must be able to present the human case to the CEO with every expectation that the CEO will respectfully listen and honor those considerations commonly dismissed as "soft." I've spoken with way too many CHROs who are afraid to even approach their CEOs with a complex, non-quantifiable conversation. They just assume that the CEOs would not be open to undertaking the challenge of understanding the human experience behind the business narrative. Consequently, the CEO doesn't have the chance to learn a new perspective. Or the CHRO approaches the CEO so timidly that the stage is set for an unbalanced conversation where the outcome is doomed to failure at the outset. And it's essential that the CHRO translates the complex human issues into observable organizational outcomes, i.e., the impact on the business.

Likewise, the CHRO is committed to operating in alignment with our shared values. Even if there is some exposure and risk attached to that position. All the CHRO rock stars I have met over time will tell me that in order to do their jobs fully, they must be prepared to lose their jobs on any given day. If it's a choice between their paycheck and taking a stand for what's right, they will take that stand.

Am I likely to fire a CHRO who has the temerity to tell me what I don't want to hear? Of course not. I might react emotionally, even angrily. I'm human. But in the context of the epic relationship, because I know that my people partner is prepared to tell me the truth, I also know that he will do what it takes to ensure our shared vision is realized. He will tell me everything I need to know. For good or ill. I may not like it. But I know he won't hold back. And that certainty in our relationship promotes trust between us.

Wise CEOs know they must draw from a wide variety of resources to help them lead their companies toward a bright future. Powerful influence comes from all around: books and Boards of Directors, other leaders we meet at conferences, consultants on occasion, the talent from throughout our entire organization of individual contributors and our inner circle of C's (financial, marketing, public affairs, all those "chiefs" who promise delivery of the highest-level advice).

CEOs who are blessed with a CHRO whom they can trust utterly, and with whom respect is a freely flowing, two-way dynamic, have the advantage of working with a true partner in the service of a shared vision. Often that vision is one that only the two of them can fully comprehend. And, as a team of two, they move the company forward toward an ineffable, people-driven reality that the numbers professionals will be able to quantify only later. It's a sparkling loyal partnership and a creative chemistry that I wish for every CEO and for every CHRO to experience in their careers. If they could only find each other.

Chapter 5
Are You An Accidental Soul-Sucking CEO?

I HAVE TO admit it. I am, frankly, quite baffled. For the last 20 years, and all around the world, we CEOs have invested untold millions into the question: "What does it take to have an engaged workplace culture?" We've bought books, retained consultants, rolled out surveys, looked deep into the hearts and minds of the people who work for us. We know how crucial it is to having talent who love working for us and who will offer discretionary effort and innovation. And introductions to their friends. We even know how to quantify all this stuff.

We are at the leading edge of an historic conversation. Our predecessors—the generations who ran the factories and cracked the whips—would look at us and our workplaces in awe. We know better than anyone at any time in the history of humans what it takes to create a workplace where people want to come to work, joyfully invest their efforts and talents into a cause greater than themselves, and then go home happy to children who are learning from their examples.

And yet we're still screwing it up. Gallup—which has made it its business to track these kinds of numbers—reports that 51% of American employees are actively looking for a job. Elsewhere. Do you know what that means on a global scale? As historically smart as we are in this whole engagement conversation, more human beings than ever before are actively seeking to leave their current employer and find fulfillment with another one.

It occurs to me that Amazon Prime and Costco have a better customer retention rate with their discretionary paid memberships than employers throughout the world have with their employees. If retail operations can more reliably keep their discretionary relationships with people who have to pay for that relationship than we can with our employees, who earn their livelihood with us, we need to take a serious look at how we're creating the environment for those relationships.

It Lands On the CEO's Door Step

Gallup statistics continue to be grim. According to its latest report, the cost of employees who are either non-engaged or actively disengaged amounts to between $960 billion and $1.2 trillion globally. Employees tell us that the relationship they want from their supervisor is one of being a coach, not a boss. They want clear expectations, accountability, a "rich purpose," ongoing feedback and, well, coaching. Only 50% report that they know what's expected of them on a daily basis; only 41% say that their actual work aligns with their formal job description (i.e., the job they signed up for in the first place). Only 44% say that they can see a connection between what they do and their company's objectives.

Those who report positively in all these areas show true returns on the investment in engagement efforts. They are anywhere between three and four times more likely to be engaged than their frustrated counterparts. When it comes to return on investment, pretty soon that adds up some real money.

The problem here is that the responsibility is conventionally assigned to the direct supervisors of employees. They're the ones who receive the reports, who are made to study the online dashboard dials and stoplights. They have to go to the trainings, and then report up line to their managers annually to account for why that needle hasn't budged. Their supervisors are doing the same. And their leaders are doing likewise. Up, up, up the org chart this accountability goes.

In the meantime, they're all receptive to calls from headhunters. Including the brain trust on your organizational development team.

The one who really should be studying how to move that needle is, well, you. While your OD department might be working so diligently to refine the behaviors of your managers to staunch the flow of your expensively acquired talent, it might be *your* office that is sucking the joy, vision, and dedication from your tribe.

Why do I use the expression "soul-sucking?" That's how it feels, especially when an organization that promotes itself as being committed to an engaged culture is led by a CEO who is unfocused, unserious, unkind, or simply doesn't get it. It's more than simply clumsy leadership. It's a breach of promise. And it makes your entire tribe feel depleted and dispirited.

How to Be a Soul-Sucking CEO

As I travel the world, leading what we call our *tribe*, I also am invited to give speeches and advise our customers and partners. I see a fervent desire to create workplace cultures that emulate the collaborative, supportive environment celebrated at WD-40 Company. And I'm gratified to be able to help them when I can.

But I am also continually surprised to see an almost entrenched, dated attitude that CEOs have toward their people and their culture. It's the only way I can explain the demoralizing engagement statistics that research companies such as Gallup serve up to us annually. With everything we now know about how to create engaging cultures, if your employees are suffering disengagement, I can only assume that you're doing this on purpose.

Since time is money, I thought I'd lend you a hand and help you further your mission of creating and sustaining a corporate culture that will drive your talent out your doors—preferably in the direction of my company. If you want to be a soul-sucking CEO, this is how you do it:

You Have No Compelling Purpose

As it turns out, having a clearly defined purpose that speaks to the hearts and minds of employees is actually critical to creating an engaged culture where your people know they belong among kindred spirits who are passionate about serving a cause larger than themselves.

In his 2018 annual letter to CEOs, Larry Fink, Chairman and CEO of global investment company, BlackRock, Inc., wrote: "To prosper over time, every company must not only deliver financial performance but also show how it makes a positive contribution to society. Without a sense of purpose, no company, either public or private, can achieve its full potential. It will lose the license to operate from key stakeholders. Demonstrate the leadership and clarity that will drive not only [your] own investment returns but also the prosperity and security of [your] fellow citizens."

Purpose-driven, passionate people guided by values create amazing outcomes. At WD-40 Company, we know that having a purpose is highly motivating. Having a purpose absolutely rewards people who are driven by the need to make a contribution bigger than themselves.

There is a psychological, physical advantage to having a true purpose. Purpose is soul-enriching, not soul-sucking. Purpose motivates people to feel part of something where they believe that they are making a difference.

When our tribe members at WD-40 come to work, they ask themselves, "What am I going to do today?" Their answer: "I'm going to create something positive for someone. I'm going to solve a problem. I'm going to make something work better. I'm going to create an opportunity. I'm going to cause a positive lasting memory for someone."

That's much more motivating than saying, "I'm going to go to work today and I'm going to sell a can of chemicals." Don't you think?

The opposite of having a purpose isn't just neutral. If you have no compelling purpose, it's an active disadvantage in the sense that there's a vacuum in focus and direction. That vacuum is going to be filled by absolutely the wrong things. You'll find yourself creating unsuccessful products that don't serve your customers. You'll have a workplace of people treating each other in a way that's shabby and disrespectful. The vacuum creates space for rumor mongering, inter-relationship suspicions and conflicts, and other destructive issues.

Your Company Has No Positive Values

Without positive values, your people will require micro-management and consistent course correction. They will be made to feel fundamentally wrong from the minute they turn off their alarm clock in the morning to the time they drag their depleted bodies back up the front walk to their house in the evening. Without values they can't be trusted to make decisions on their own. And they will know it. They are exposed, and they know their company is exposed. Any day some horrible headline about some unethical behavior committed by an executive will cause the whole company to come crashing down.

Values create freedom for purpose-driven talent to do their work well and independently. They are the written reminders of behaviors that we want within the business that protect both the people and the business. They also give people the freedom to be able to make decisions without having to beg permission up the hierarchy all the time.

A strong culture based on values also sets the stage for innovation and marketplace advantage because you now have employees who are not using their precious brain cells worrying about unexpected ways they might mess up. They're free to innovate and create market-differentiating, competitive ideas.

Having strong values protects you from measuring and rewarding the wrong behaviors and objectives. At WD-40 Company, we include values as part of our talent management system. Values override fiscal results when we evaluate our tribe members' performance.

The worst thing that can happen in an organization is someone getting really good results and violating values. Inevitably, people conclude that "it's results at all costs and values don't matter." That will kill your company over the long term. It demoralizes your people, depletes energy, squanders confidence, burns up the sense of belonging inside your culture. It creates friction among tribe members. People start doing really bad things; they hurt each other and your customers, just to get results.

You Let Your Ego Override Your Empathy

Instead of treating people with respect and dignity, instead of showing vulnerability and humility, you might as well put a sign on your office door (always closed, of course) that reads: "I am the King of the World. Everyone bow down." You separate yourself from those you lead.

You don't take the time to truly understand what your people need to stay inspired and motivated. You don't know what they need to be whole in their entire lives, to feel fulfilled in every aspect of their experiences. It's all about you. Which is exactly as you feel it should be. Because you are, after all, the King of the World. You worked hard to achieve your position on the pedestal. And you're not about to step down now.

People with ego always want to speak first. They want to tell; they don't want to ask. They want to own every idea, even—or especially—if it means taking credit away from the person who originated it.

Marshall Goldsmith talks about "adding too much value." As leaders we want to contribute our influence to projects that our tribe members own. Just a tweak here or a tweak there gives you the ego satisfaction of adding your golden touch. What you have done is dramatically reduce the enthusiasm of your staff member. Your ego tells you that you must have your stamp on it.

You Are Short-term And Reaction Driven

The vision-crushing ritual of quarterly earnings is not the measure of long-term success in any organization. Being continuously driven by the reward of the short term will suck the soul of the organization. Efforts to build an enduring, positive, and effective culture take years to make a difference. There is no such thing as grabbing the "low-hanging fruit," when the task is planting and nourishing a beautiful tree over time.

Focus on the short term and you'll cripple any ability for your people to plan confidently for the future, for both your business and their family. You will be helping your talent destroy their careers while you destroy their faith in your company. And then they take that feeling home to their families where they struggle to raise hopeful, empowered children.

You Create a Culture Where People Are Driven By Fear Of Their Managers

Fear is the most disabling emotion we have. Yet bad things happen in companies. It's just a fact of life. When your people are afraid to try new things, make a mistake now and then, despite the best of intentions, fear precludes creativity and freedom.

Remember the Learning Moment? It's the positive or negative outcome of any situation that must be openly and freely shared to benefit all. Anyone can openly say, "I had a learning moment, here's what happened, and here's how it will be better tomorrow." Or "I had a learning moment, and here's what happened, here's the great result I got, and here's what I want to share."

The number one responsibility of a leader is to be both a student and a teacher. And then pass both those values on to the entire organization. No one should be afraid of reprisals from their managers for making innocent mistakes. If you take the fear of the result out, you create a culture that's more open to learning.

Inject fear of sharing critical learnings with managers and teams, and you'll successfully suck the soul out of your cherished talent.

You Don't Keep Promises

One of the ways you destroy trust immediately is to not do what you say you're going to do. If you have a track record of breaking promises, it says two soul-sucking things to employees:

1. **Anyone's word inside the corporate culture doesn't amount to much.** Not only is the CEO's word worthless, no one is expected to be accountable for their commitments. Breaking promises is a culturally accepted norm.

2. **If your employees are on the receiving end of broken promises, the unspoken message here is that they aren't worthy of the leader's respect.** That's also soul-sucking. The only way your people can continue to function inside this culture is simply to not expect honorable interaction from their leadership and coworkers. Expectations are too high. Their hearts will break. Then they go home and kick the dog.

You Hoard Information

Knowledge is power. We all know that. You can capitalize on that power by either sharing the knowledge throughout your organization, or let your ego compel you to hoard information. With all the critical knowledge safely tucked away, you are now truly king of the hill because you know everything.

And they (whoever "they" are at any given moment) know nothing. Your ego is more important than your people. Keeping critical information to yourself is your superpower. And your ego wants you to hang onto it.

Employees who suspect that their CEO is withholding valuable information experience the slow leaking of their spirits, confidence and dedication to your company's success. That's because they don't feel like *their* success is your number one priority. A true soul-enriching leader is intent upon helping each person step into the best version of their personal self every day. And that requires a full, respectful sharing of the information necessary for your people to perform at their top potential. Every day.

No, You're Not Crazy

As I consider this list of soul-sucking CEO behaviors, it makes me sad to reflect on the fact that these are common in workplaces still today. Even though we all know that this kind of leadership is toxic, depleting, and company destroying. We see the damage this kind of behavior causes over and over again as companies spectacularly flame out, and many of these kinds of leaders even end up having to pay their debts to society behind bars.

I also have to ask myself how it is that leaders are allowed to behave this way, even with the first soul-sucking action—whether it's a lie, an emotional outburst, a broken promise, or some kind of Machiavellian mind game designed to test the loyalty of one direct report over another. These kinds of behaviors start out so small, so inconsequential, no one wants to speak up or out. But the intensity gradually builds up over time.

People become like the proverbial boiled frog. All over the world, millions of talented and otherwise high-value people trudge to work daily, with their hearts broken and their faith in themselves crushed into powder. And they wonder if they're the ones who are crazy, and if somehow they have done something to deserve this experience. Or, if maybe, this is the way they should one day lead as they scratch and crawl their way up the career ladder themselves. What a loss to the world this becomes.

There Are No Accidents

The title of this chapter is, "Are You an *Accidental* Soul-Sucking CEO?" Now that you know the many ways a disengaged culture can be manifested from the top, "I didn't know," or "I didn't mean to," can no longer be true. As the CEO, nothing in your portfolio should be allowed to be assigned to "accident."

Two quotes come to mind at this point. One is slightly older than the other.

Back in 384 BC, Aristotle was quoted as saying, "Pleasure in the job puts perfection in the work." Our job as the CEO is to put pleasure in the job for our employees, not suck the soul out of our people. The question as to whether it's our job to make our employees happy comes in and out of fashion over the decades. But, based on Gallup's findings, it would seem that Aristotle might have been on to something. In my own personal experience, pleasure in my job empowers higher quality in the work I do. And I see evidence of same in my tribe members. It's not about making people happy. It's about creating an opportunity for meaningful work, which is in itself a pleasure to perform. And then the result is a company that meets—or even surpasses—all its critical goals.

More recently, Stephen Covey said, "I am not a product of my circumstances. I am a product of my decisions."

In this particular case, the decision I put to you is whether you will commit to being the leader where your joyful workplace culture begins. If you choose not to, that is certainly your prerogative. Just bear in mind that 51% of the people you pass in your hallways or meet in your cafeteria might be looking for a new job.

We at WD-40 Company would be delighted to consider their resumes. And we have a 93% engagement rate. Not to brag. I just want to give you an idea who might be welcoming aboard your best talent. Correction: Your former best talent. Now they're our best talent.

Your decision.

Chapter 6
When Caring Collides With Candor

THE LEARNING NEVER stops as you climb the ranks of corporate leadership. You acquire the technical skills and industry insights necessary to stay ahead of the game. And they just require refresher courses now and then to keep your saw sharpened. But the higher up the ranks you ascend, the demand for technical acumen makes way for the increased need to broaden and deepen your people skills. Those lessons never seem to end.

In fact, it often feels that you're being required by repeat the same lesson, but each time at perhaps a different level. As you rise, more and more people depend on you to be wise, with your emotional reactions tempered with perspective and proportion. You subscribe to the belief that it's your job as the leader to create a company culture where your people—your tribe—feel safe to focus on their work, feel fulfilled and then go home at night to their families feeling happy and optimistic about the future. This means that you have to find that balance between being an inspiring, even demanding, leader who ignites high performance standards company-wide and being a *caring* human being whose own example creates an emotionally healthy work environment where people do their best because they want to and they feel supported by their leaders.

That requires a certain amount of emotional health. And, quite frankly, none of us can be emotionally healthy all the time. We each bring our baggage to the workplace (I'm fond of saying, however, that I prefer to leave my baggage at the station). And our tribe members don't always experience our best moments. As sincerely as we may try to rise above our emotions, inevitably we put the wrong foot forward at times. And, oops, here comes another go at the lesson you thought you had already nailed.

For me, the lesson is a very specific one—I'm learning it all the time: How to be caring ("tender hearted") and candid ("tough minded") at the same time. I struggle with this dichotomy more than any other leadership challenge because I know myself well enough to know that I can quickly go to either extreme of this continuum—benefitting neither the business nor the individual I'm working with.

At WD-40 Company, we want to create positive, lasting memories with everyone we do business with—both the customers and all our tribe members. In our role as leaders, this means that our primary desire in every interaction with our people is to help them be better at the work they do. Being a leader is not about inflating our egos or exerting some kind of dominance. And so ideally, we enter into coaching conversations with a humble heart, even though the circumstance might require a certain amount of toughness.

But because we're all human, with our own frustrations and emotional needs, we must be ever vigilant to make sure that our spirit of authentic caring doesn't morph into indulging our need to release negative energy on the tribe member we're supposed to be supporting. Even in the most difficult conversations that require more candor than caring, leaders have to stay on top of that impulse—no matter how well-intentioned they may be going into the meeting.

I have to watch myself almost every day. Because of my overwhelming caring for my tribe, I can very easily stay in the tender-hearted realm, where I become soft to the point that I'm no longer helping the person I'm coaching. I become overly compassionate, losing sight of my duty to help that tribe member achieve the best outcome for all of us.

At the other end of the spectrum, I have to admit that I am quite capable of becoming too tough if I drop my self-awareness along the way. I am at risk of allowing my ego to take over, and I feel anger, resentment, betrayal, and a degree of negativity toward the tribe member that that person doesn't deserve. Because I'm aware of this tendency, I am also aware of my inclination to withdraw and avoid the difficult conversation altogether. And that helps no one either.

Whether your nature is to reside on the soft-hearted end of the continuum or on the tough end, you are abdicating your responsibility as a tribe leader.

But you are human too. And you both deserve and require the emotional support necessary to rise to your leadership role. To that end, I would like to offer you these key considerations that will help shape your temperament as you enter difficult, but essential, conversations:

Always being aware of the power of your leadership position. Don't lose sight of the fact that no matter how wounded, betrayed, or cheated you may be feeling at the time, the wrong word from you, delivered in a thoughtless, emotional way, could devastate your tribe member.

There are at least two equally legitimate interpretations of any incident that might precipitate a difficult conversation. Harness your own emotionalized reaction by quietly and sincerely inviting your tribe member to explain the alternative interpretation. Three words, "help me understand," will not only buy you time to regain control over your own reactions but also give your tribe member the chance to be heard and understood.

Always assume positive intent. In most cases, people don't come to work with the intention of destroying their company or compromising an initiative they're working on. They are not saboteurs. By and large, they're just people doing their best. And screwing up now and then. So are you. There's something you two have in common.

Hold front of mind that this difficult conversation carries with it more value than merely resolving the crisis immediately at hand. This is an opportunity for the two of you to achieve an enriched bond of trust and deepened relationship. Assuming that both of you want to continue your working relationship, this encounter will nurture the respect and understanding between you two. And you will demonstrate both your own sincerity and vulnerability that will strengthen the health of your entire tribal culture.

In our tribe, we are safe to assume that we are all reasonable people, sharing the same values, and equipped with the same information that is essential to serve our company. We are also all learning to be better performers. And better people. Even the CEO.

Part II:
How It's Going

Chapter 7
2020: Look Back in Gratitude

AS I'M WRITING this article, we're closing out the first year of Covid-19; deep into February 2021. We had such high hopes for change by now. But schools are still closed to some degree or another. Expectations of vaccine efficacy have been questioned. The one-two shot was supposed to get us back to some kind of normal within a month or two. Well, Anthony Fauci is now predicting the Fall of 2021. And a third shot might be on the horizon, not to mention the mention of booster shots.

Recommendations for mask-wearing have been doubled—even in some cases tripled. (I think that three-mask idea is still said in jest. But it's hard to tell anymore. Anyway, the jokes aren't funny.) It was only six weeks ago—as of this writing—that all of us were looking forward to the turning of the calendar from 2020 to 2021, like that would be some magical dateline where 2020 would give up and hand over reins to 2021, saying, "Here, time to make it all better." And 2021 just laughed.

The question must be asked: How are you liking 2021 so far? We had such high hopes for the new year, especially given the adverse circumstances we thought we were leaving in our rearview mirror. But now Facebook posts from ordinary individuals all over the world are including such messages as "hold my beer." And there's an updated Gary Larson cartoon featuring two burning buildings, one marked 2020, the other 2021. Firefighters watch as a would-be rescuee from 2020 bounces off their trampoline and dives headlong into the flaming window in building 2021. (After all these decades of retirement, Larson sure picked up his pen again at just the right time, didn't he? The Millennials and Gen Zers are in for a treat. A sardonic one, to be sure, but a treat just the same.)

I know. It seems like a weird time to be talking about gratitude right now, doesn't it? "Counter-intuitive," as they say in the impressive buzzword circles. In private conversations, friends talk about their gratitude journals. Some have just started one, in an attempt to take the edge of mounting anxiety. And build on what's good in life. Others are into their 20th year, devotedly filling up one volume after another.

What might be in your personal journal? Family, of course. Premium coffee and tea that are still affordable? The travel coffee mug that you still use to keep your morning drink hot, even though your morning commute is bedroom to bathroom to home office (or dining room table)? A reasonably reliable paycheck? Streaming movies on demand? That Christmas cactus that miraculously came back to life, when the only reason that it didn't end up in the garbage is because you just kept putting it off? Electricity? Access to a piano that doesn't require electricity? A choice of vaccines? Seeing your name on the waiting list for the vaccine? Friends who disagree with you but love you anyway? Bedroom slippers and the fact that you can still attend Zoom meetings dressed for business from the waist up? The fact that you have cultivated the personal habit of *never* assuming that your video camera is off?

Gratitude also comes in the form of comparing what we have now with what we didn't have in the past. It's safe to say that most of the most senior executives today remember a time when they didn't have Internet, and now they do. But, astoundingly, there are executives who remember a time when they didn't have plumbing, and now they do. Or they grew up in violently dysfunctional families, and now their homelife is serene. Just comparing and contrasting between past and present gives us plenty of material to feel good about.

We are reminded by the gratitude experts that we benefit by cultivating gratitude for all aspects of our lives—things and events both large and small. Everyone has something to be grateful for. Even today, in these times of extreme anxiety and social divisiveness. So maybe it's not so counterintuitive after all. Future generations who will one day have the good fortune to read today's gratitude journals of their ancestors (who would be us right now) will be in for an eyeful. Hopefully, their own lives will have advanced so far in abundance, progress, and comfort (thanks in no small measure to the sacrifices we're making today, by the way), that they'll exhale a breath of gratitude that the quality of life characterized by 2020-2021 is long since gone.

So that's a snapshot of our personal excursions into the gratitude experience. How can CEOs and other senior leaders leverage gratitude as a competitive advantage that sets the stage for future growth? Is it weird—maybe even bogus—for a CEO of a global company, like me, for instance, to look back on 2020 and consider what there might be to be grateful for on a grander scale than our personal notebooks destined to be reviewed by future generations? As someone who makes a point of handwriting thank-you notes to tribe members, I can tell you from first-hand experience that gratitude is actually an executive superpower. Not only in how he or she relates to tribe members, but also in how gratitude fosters expansive thinking and innovation. Gratitude is a personal experience.

But it is also supremely powerful on an organizational level. And it's accessible. You need only to choose to apply the philosophy of gratitude as a corporate leadership perspective. In his foreword to the book *Leading with Gratitude: Eight Leadership Practices for Extraordinary Business Results* (by Chester Elton and Adrian Gostick), Marshall Goldsmith wrote: "Gratitude is a mental state that a) you can most easily decide to feel, b) has the most immediate effect on improving your well-being, and c) is going to have a remarkable impact on your ability to lead other people. The challenge is to remember to do it!"

These days, the real challenge is to remember to do it in the face of hard evidence that lures us in the direction of believing that there's not much to be grateful for at all. Yes, 2020 was filled with some tragedy. There is no denying that. But most of us who are here today to even look back on 2020 to any degree can take up the leadership challenge and truly acknowledge that 2020 came with gifts.

(As I just wrote this line, I'm reminded of Phra Phuttha Maha Suwanna Patimakon, the gold Buddha statue in Bangkok, which was encased in stucco for centuries. At 5,500 kg, its immense value in gold had been hidden from marauders who only saw the stucco and dismissed it as worthless. What is the value of 2020 for you as a corporate leader? Or do you only see the stucco, the pain? The loss? The uncertainty? The anxiety? Can you spot the hint of gold that is sure to lie beneath?)

And so I sat down to think it through. What do I have to be grateful for from Year 2020, which will equip me and the WD-40 Company tribe to prevail through 2021 and beyond? Come what may? Here's what I came up with:

Gratitude for Vicissitudes

Have you heard the story of the farmer and his dizzying round of episodes of bad luck and good luck? As with every story that has survived the centuries via the oral tradition, it has multiple versions. The one I will summarize here comes from *Think Like a Monk: Train Your Mind for Peace and Purpose Every Day* by Jay Shetty.

There was once a farmer whose horse ran away. "Oh! How unlucky," cried his brother. "Good thing, bad thing, who knows?" answered the farmer. (I'm thinking that maybe his wife might have had a different attitude about the whole episode, though. Just a gut feeling.)

Horse comes back, this time in the company of a mare. "Oh! How lucky," cries the brother. "Good thing. Bad thing. Who knows?" says the farmer.

Son tries to tame the mare, falls off, breaks his leg. Well, you can guess the rest.

Broken leg protects the son from being conscripted into the military.

Shetty sums up the story with the lesson, "Don't judge the moment."

When you're the CEO who is responsible for being able to see around corners and make billion-dollar decisions accordingly, there are board members who won't appreciate that line, "Good thing, bad thing, who knows?" They may or may not judge the moment, but they sure will judge you if you drew on that bit of wisdom and announced it during an earnings call.

And yet, as much as senior executives are counted on by thousands of people (employees, investors, customers, to start with) to make wise and right decisions, we make those decisions based on *known knowns,* as Donald Rumsfeld said when he described his approach to strategic planning. But even if we think we know the knowns, we are taken by surprise when the world is turned upside down like a snow globe. Our constituents may still look to us to make the right decisions given the changed sets of circumstances. But we know better than anyone that good news and bad news often switch identities before they present themselves to us.

Don't do what the farmer did—taking the flood of ups and downs in passive stride. People who count on your active optimism and resilience would prefer a more energetic, proactive approach to the *known unknowns.* But you can still be grateful for the *unknowable unknowns,* holding the posture that it's not the circumstance that will make all the difference at the end of the day, but the way you decide to respond to it. You'll be in for a surprise, to be sure. With deft handling of your reactions to the unknowables, there is sure to be a benefit hidden in that room full of question marks.

Which, of course, reminds me of the punch line to one of my favorite stories: "There's a pony in there somewhere!" said the optimistic boy, joyful at the sight of his room filled with horse manure.

Gratitude for Purpose

I don't especially enjoy talking about myself (I'd rather tell you about how wonderful the WD-40 Company tribe is). But one of my favorite stories I like to tell is the one in which I discovered my purpose. As these things happen—like finding love or happiness—discovering my purpose happened in a single moment when I was least expecting it. I was in the air, flying over the South Pacific from California to Australia, filling up the hours by reading a book by the Dalai Lama. I read these words, "The purpose of life is to make people happy. If you can't make them happy, at least don't hurt them." From that moment, my role as a leader clarified, and this purpose became my North Star in every decision I make.

(What does *happy* mean, from the perspective of the CEO's relationship to the tribe? Good question. But for the moment, I'd like to offer the perspective that to be a CEO whose purpose is to make people happy is a servant leadership stance. But *happy*, if thoughtlessly taken to extremes, can diminish a CEO from servant to servile. This is not an, "Everybody gets a pony!" proposition. The CEO is tasked with making tough choices that affect the day-to-day life experience of all the tribe members. From the tribe members' perspective, the experience of happy must be drawn from doing work that is meaningful to them, in a culture that they can depend on to be consistent and reasonably predictable, with fellow tribe members whom they trust, in a way that's consistent with the company's values. Not everyone will be happy with the way their day plays out. But over time, from the big picture perspective, when the CEO does it reasonably right, the tribe can trust that all decisions are made for the greater good, for now and for the future. And that is a grand purpose right there.)

That commitment helped me through 2020 when I was working through decisions on keeping the company on track for our identified mission, regardless of external circumstances. It also kept my passion alive in conditions that might have otherwise depleted my energy, creativity, and faith in the future. If I wake up every morning thinking about selling oil, I would lose my passion and momentum. I get up every day reflecting on what Barry Wehmiller Chairman and CEO Bob Chapman says, "Everybody who comes to work is someone's precious child." (Or, of course, someone's precious parent.)

During 2020 I agonized over the fear of potentially having to let people go. I have a responsibility, even a relationship, with everyone who works at WD-40 Company. If we bring a new member into the tribe, we have to be confident that we can sustain our new tribe member. While I can't responsibly say that we will never lay anyone off, I can say that since October 7, 1997, the day I was honored with the opportunity to lead our tribe, we have never laid anyone off due to any financial crisis.

In the early days of Covid, it was the intensity of the uncertainty that kept me awake at night. I chose to take a pragmatic, optimistic approach—an optimism based on a level of understanding that was at least viable and acceptable. From that position, I've been able to serve the company as well as our tribe. I am able to live my purpose.

Gratitude for Our Company Values

I mentioned values above as I was expanding on how I activate my purpose on a daily basis with my tribe. From the tribe's perspective, decisions and behaviors are examples of our values in action. These examples show us what the values look like as they play out daily. They also accumulate to ultimately create our culture. The more we behave and makes decisions according to our values, the more our culture is created in a dependable, consistent way. Which ultimately frees up our tribe members to invest their intellectual and emotional energies into creating a company culture that is literally friction-free. I've simplified this concept in the following formula:

Culture = (Values + Behavior) x Consistency

Our company values are the guardrails of our culture. With the guardrails in place, we can move forward as freely as we desire, without the friction, drag, and anxiety that come from confusion when we don't know what's expected of us. Enhancing my own personal purpose is the Number One Value of our company, which is, "We value doing the right thing." What was the right thing from Day One of our Covid-19 adventure? To take care of the safety and well-being of the tribe.

After that, our values go in this order:

> "We value creating positive, lasting memories in all of our relationships."
> "We value making it better than it is today."
> "We value succeeding as a tribe while excelling as individuals."
> "We value owning it and passionately acting on it."
> "We value sustaining the WD-40 Company economy."

I don't even worry about manifesting the last value, because if we all take ownership of doing the right thing by our fellow tribe members in accordance with Values One through Five, the sixth value will naturally unfold, even in a global economy ravaged by Covid-19. We never strayed from our values and we were rewarded by the realization of our value of sustaining the WD-40 Company economy.

Gratitude for Our Collaborative Culture

A few months ago, I was leading a highly productive, congenial global zoom meeting that went smoothly, leavened with laughter. On a whim, at the end of the meeting I asked the participants to contribute a single word each thought best described their experience of the meeting. Once we plugged all the words into one of those word cloud programs, this is the word that stood out beyond all the others: Collaboration.

That pleased me no end. Here we were, all alone, altogether, all around the world, after months of very strange isolation. And yet we were still able to achieve the joyful mind-meld that is the result of years of consistent, trusting allegiance to each other.

Our last engagement survey showed that 98% of our employees love to tell people that they work for WD-40 Company. I have no doubt that they are as proud of our products as I am. And that we are all very much aware of the many ways that what we do and make create a better life for millions of people around the globe. But I am also very certain that we make life better for our WD-40 Company tribe by our consistent culture of open, trusting, friction-free sharing of information and ideas throughout the organization, up and down the ranks, all around the planet.

Gratitude for Data Points

"A few more steps and we'll be safe in the Fire Swamp!"

"We'll never survive!"

"Nonsense. You're only saying that because no one ever has."

Fans of the epic Rob Reiner film, *The Princess Bride*, will recognize those lines instantly. It's an exchange between Princess Buttercup and her hero Westley (traveling incognito as the Dread Pirate Roberts). Into the Fire Swamp they run, escaping the pursuit of the evil prince who wants to marry her (or, as *Princess Bride* geeks would say, *mawwy*). Inside the swamp, they quickly discover its three dangers: fire spurts, lightning sand, and the dreaded Rodents of Unusual Size (ROUS's, for those in the know). Instead of allowing these hazards to demoralize them utterly (which would have been entirely understandable), Westley and Buttercup rationally made note of them, what signaled their presence, and kept moving through the swamp. Granted, some scratches, some blood, a lot of sand, and a burned hem—but they prevailed.

What was the secret to their survival? As life-threatening as those three dangers were, Westley and Buttercup coolly took in the data points, without allowing their perilous situation to define their destiny and pull down their spirits.

The year 2020 was our Fire Swamp throughout the world. The hazardous journey inarguably threatened—and, in some cases, destroyed—the health and prospects of businesses that deserved to be here today. There is no diminishing or ignoring the tragedy and the devastation suffered by hundreds of thousands of enterprises that were healthy in December 2019.

But those of us who made it all the way through emerged with an understanding of our own landscape of hazards that will stay with us into the future, unless we coolly acknowledge their existence and address them now. An underserved market? A product line that has outlived its relevance to its customers? Labor issues that must be resolved quickly? A supply chain that depends way too much on the good will of a single nation? All these hazards are easily padded over, ignored, hidden, and underappreciated when times are good. But when you're running for your life through the Fire Swamp of bad times, that's when their negative impact will have dimensions of "unusual size."

How is it possible to be grateful for the Fire Swamp of 2020, when we're surrounded by the ashes of businesses that deserved to still be here with us? Our reduced circumstances and focus revealed to all of us the unique set of data points that showed us where our own particular hazards were, where to step, what to avoid, what to fix, what to create to be responsive to our new future. We only had to pay attention, take note, and take action to the data points.

Gratitude for Being Forced Off Our Esses

There's a phrase going around these days that goes like this:

Soft times make soft people; soft people make hard times; hard times make hard people; hard people make soft times.

This is another way of describing the S curve (or *growth curve*) that Whitney Johnson describes in her book, *Disrupt Yourself: Master Relentless Change and Speed Up Your Learning Curve* (which is one of my favorites, by the way). While she initially describes the growth curve in the context of some kind of innovation in the market space that causes extreme disruption, the growth curve can also depict what happens to us and our business model when caught by surprise by an upheaval. Imagine a capital S with a very long upward line. At the bottom and top of that long vertical line are two horizontal lines—very much like a serif S that you can see anywhere. Those flat lines represent plateaus of rest, recovery, and sometimes just living life day-by-day, doing what you've always done. You're comfortable but your development isn't anything to write home about. Then suddenly, zoom! Upward you go again! Disruption!

"Part of the reason disruption can be so hard to spot is the timing; the growth curve can look totally flat for years, then spike upward very steeply," she wrote. "As the pace of disruptive innovation quickens and you are in the midst of a crashing wave, what is unsettling can also be an amazing ride. Disrupting yourself is critical to avoiding stagnation [and] being overtaken … and fast-tracking your personal and career growth."

The year 2020 roared us up the steep incline of the S-curve, and it was a harrowing ride, to say the least. My hope for you is that your steep ride has ceased, at least for the immediate time being so you can catch your breath. Ideally, you're on the next level plateau, holding on for a moment, letting your adrenaline levels return to normal. But the ride's not done. Year 2021 will send you zooming up the next incline. While you're gathering your wits about you right now, reflect on the experience that 2020 gave you and be grateful for the last ride. It will give you confidence that you will survive the next innovation—or upheaval—and arrive at new heights as a reward. While that experience isn't guaranteed to be a beneficial thing, a philosophy of gratitude will improve your odds of a more positive, expansive outcome, with new possibilities that you might have overlooked before.

Gratitude for Grace

Back in January 2020, before the Covid-19 news fully came crashing down on the globe, the planet was on the move. Front doors were opening, closing, opening again as parents went to work and kids rushed off to school in the morning. Car engines fired up in the frosty mornings. In many parts of the world, impatient commuters cursed under their breath as they discovered that they had to scrape the windshields before they could get a move-on. People sprinted down concourses for their flights—reluctantly passing the coffee stands. And traffic control screens were crammed with those silhouettes of planes, often overlapping, on their way somewhere essential to the people onboard.

Then in the span of just a couple of days, front doors opened one last time, closed again, and stayed closed. Flight reservations were cancelled. Flights were cancelled. And one by one those little airplane silhouettes disappeared from the air traffic control screens. The screens were empty. The streets were empty. The office buildings were empty. The homes were full of people looking at each other and wondering, "What do we do now?"

A year has passed and we're slowly cranking up the machine again. And, much to our surprise, we're making mistakes in activities we used to do so much we did them unconsciously. It's like learning to walk again. Muscles and coordination we used to take for granted, we have to patiently re-educate ourselves to use again. That's a strange and unexpected upward climb of a growth curve we didn't expect to see.

Whitney Johnson tells this story in an exclusive interview for this piece:

"I think about moving into 2021 as an experiment, instead of putting pressure on myself to get it right. We're just learning all over again. When you take your ego out of it, it makes all the difference.

"A couple of weeks ago I had to travel again after having not traveled in eight months. Because I hadn't traveled in so long, my basic system was out of practice. And I was well into my trip when I realized I had forgotten my watch charger and critical clothing. This is rookie-level inefficiency, not something that someone who travels as much as I do would do.

"I had to stop and remind myself not to get angry at myself, and I'm not going to get angry at anyone else. I would use this as an opportunity to practice resilience. I'm a really goal-oriented person and not having my watch to track and record my physical activity was really frustrating. Especially since I was about to close in on a milestone. But I resolved to not go to the Apple store to get a replacement charger. And I wasn't going to buy new clothes. I would practice resilience and self-compassion. And just make do with what I had.

"Was it messy? Yes. Inconvenient? Sure. Frustrating? Could have been. But really, those things we could automatically depend on and plan for last year just aren't in the picture anymore. At least not in the way they used to be.

"Going into 2021, we have to give ourselves a lot of grace, make room for experimentation, and disorderliness and distraction. Two years ago, we might have been mortified if a small child was disrupting our Zoom call. Now, well, it's just the way it is."

Gratitude for the Companionship on This Crazy Ride

Chester Elton, one of the authors of *Leading With Gratitude*, says, "Being a CEO who is able to look at this array of realities for good and for ill, and still find an upside to the story, that's the ideal. This is how leaders can form a tribal culture where the members can at least find stability in the shared philosophy that, 'Okay, we're all in this together.' There can be good that will come out of this.

"No, let me rephrase that. We're all in this together and isn't this exciting?"

As we learn more and more about the psychological benefits of gratitude in the way they help us expand possibilities in our own lives and careers, in our employees' lives and careers, to our companies' performance in the global market, we become more and more motivated to notice, appreciate and give grace for the mess wherever we can. So let's get started expanding our gratitude practice.

Right about here is where I normally type, "No time like the present." But not this time. No time like the past.

Like 2020.

Chapter 8
Rank Your Values to Get It Right in the Right Order

LEADERSHIP IS ABOUT making tough choices. Whatever the external circumstances surrounding our business (pandemic, global political upheaval, a rapidly changing marketplace, or even just an ordinary weekday), I think that everyone would agree with me on that truism.

But I'd also like to add that the way you organize your thinking about those tough choices is important too. It reveals the way you relate to not only your company's values, but also to the way you prioritize them hierarchically as each new tough challenge demands fresh thinking. You're making the decision-making process easier on yourself. And you're setting the stage for your people—your tribe, as I call them—to make decisions independently with confidence and expectation that even if the outcome doesn't come out quite right, you'll still stand by them. Because they followed your established values hierarchy.

Few leadership-level decisions have guaranteed outcomes, of course. But what is a guaranteed outcome is that the way we actively use our corporate values as a sort of constraining structure helps us improve our chances of making the best decision available to us. And it breathes life into our corporate culture and protects our relationship with our tribe.

This is especially the case when the external circumstances are so chaotic—like the Covid-19 pandemic, for instance—that a company and all the individuals associated with it are asking themselves, "Who am I now in the context of this new cataclysmic shift? And how must I change to be most relevant to the times without abandoning my fundamental nature?" To answer these questions, we are wise to go back to that list of what we hold most dear—our values.

It's not enough to simply have a set of values disconnected from each other, with no supporting description of how those values are manifest through actions and decisions. They must be organized—constrained, as it were—according to a hierarchy so that no valuable consideration is skipped over. Nothing is overlooked. Nothing is sacrificed—even unconsciously and well-meaningly—because individual biases overrule the discipline of the values structure. Let your values set drive your decision-making process in a hierarchical framework, and you remove time- and energy-wasting friction in your corporate culture. And you will build trust among your tribe.

Let me show you what I mean. When I speak to university business classes, I challenge them with a case study exercise that pits competing values against each other: the "right thing to do" for the business, for employees, or for management self-interest. In one proposed solution, the short-term financial returns on the risk have higher odds of being realized than longer-term scenarios.

After the class members receive the case study, I divide them into three groups. Group A gets to tackle the problem any way they want to. Total freedom. Group B must address the case study governed by the set of company values. Otherwise, they're free to strive for the solution to the case study any way they choose. Group C can also do whatever they want, but they are constrained by not only the values but also the values as they are addressed in a hierarchical system. Think of it as them pushing the problem through sieves of ever-finer mesh. Or smoothing out a wooden table using graduated grains of sandpaper.

Because this is my class, I get to decide what the values are and in what order. Naturally, I choose to use the WD-40 Company values in this order of hierarchy:

> **We value doing the right thing.** We do the right thing in serving our tribe mates, our stockholders, our customers, our products' consumers, our suppliers and even our competitors—doing what's

right according to the situation and the context. If we are honest, and if we speak and act congruently, we will be doing what is right.

We value creating positive lasting memories in all our relationships. As a result of our interactions with our tribe and stakeholders, we all will feel better at the end of the interaction than we did when we began; we will leave with a positive memory of it.

We value making it better than it is today. We strive for continual improvement. There is a special moment that occurs right at the point in time where a person gains an insight or new knowledge because of a particularly positive ... or negative ... event. We are constantly on the lookout for these "learning moments," because they are the fuel for continual improvement.

We value succeeding as a tribe while excelling as individuals. We recognize that the collective success comes first. Individual excellence is the means by which our organization succeeds. And "excellence" is defined as outstanding contribution to the whole.

We value owning it and passionately acting on it. We get our shoes dirty. We are relentless about understanding our business and our role in impacting it.

We value sustaining the WD-40 Company economy. We exist to create and protect economic value for all our tribe and stakeholders.

After I equip my students with not only these values but also a thorough understanding of how these values are expressed in action and behaviors, I send them off into their three groups to figure out a solution to the case study. By the time their allotted 20 minutes are up, the first group (the one with all the freedom) has come up with only frustration and sometimes even rancor among them. They have experienced what I call "ultimate churn." The second group (the one with values but no hierarchical structure) spent their 20 minutes arguing over which values are most important to serve first.

The third group, however, always delivers its solution first, happy as a group with the conclusion they've come to and satisfied with the outcome.

What does this repeatable experiment tell us? In an organization where you don't have a hierarchical set of values, you get wasted time, friction, and futility. You build dissent among your people, trust is destroyed, and people take on offense at a personal level. Subcultures defined by shared points of view begin to form. And these subcultures are like the antibodies that invade the petri dish of corporate culture to devour the good qualities.

Values—along with their hierarchical structure—are the constraints that free us to turn our attention, energies, and synergies to the activities that matter the most to us in the long run. They keep our culture secure and supported while we extend ourselves into unknown variables, territories, and innovations that will take us into a prosperous future. Some might consider them too binding to foster creativity, but I would like to put to you these five ways they free us to do our best work:

> **Values free us from churn.** When we think of churn, we think of lack of direction, a lot of energy invested in going around in circles (consider a washing machine or an ocean whirlpool). There is a lot of yanking about, with no clear exit point where escape can be had. As we have already discussed, churn compromises relationships and trust inside teams (not to mention all stakeholders who have a relationship with your company). Churn stops the free-flowing exchange of information because people begin to prioritize protecting themselves and their careers over the concerns and priorities of their teams and the company as a whole. Your people spend their energies and creative capacity on their self-interest instead of pursuing a solid, unified direction as indicated by your organization.

> **Values free us from regret.** Not every tough leadership decision turns out the way we want it too. That's just a fact of life. But if we are able to "show our work," so to speak, where we can demonstrate how we made our decisions according to the hierarchical structure of the pre-established values set, we can confidently stand by our efforts and say that we did our best. We can transform the disappointment into an extremely valuable Learning Moment, which will serve us as an entire tribe well into the future. The real gift of the Learning Moment is that it is an accelerator of the business

success; it's a Learning Moment that we don't have to waste time repeating as a tribe.

Values free us to attract the tribe members we want in our organization. When you can clearly articulate what is most important to your company and culture, and set up your values in such a way that your candidates can see their own values reflected in what you stand for, your selection, recruiting, and onboarding conversations reinforce and reassure all parties that they are in good company. WD-40 Company's employee opinion surveys report that 97% of our people believe their values align with the company's values. And 98% say that they are proud to say that they work for WD-40 Company. When you have that level of alignment, your interactions inside your company culture are richer, free from fear and avoidable discord.

Values free us to attract the right customers. In recent decades, we have come to appreciate the power of inviting our customers to engage with us on levels that are more emotionally evocative than simply choosing a can of oil. We stand for creating positive, lasting memories. Those memories manifest not only in the stories our customers bring to us (repairing a bike for a child, for instance), but they also show up in the message we send to our customers. They belong, for example, to a tribe whose values require a healthy product, manufactured in an environmentally and socially responsible way throughout the world. We belong to each other— company, tribe, customer. And the ground we stand on is enriched by our shared values and the stories we tell each other about how we express those values every day.

"Imagine those iconic Russian dolls—the kind that nest together, the very largest to the almost inconceivably smallest," says my mentor, Ken Blanchard, author of so many beloved books, including one everyone knows, *The One Minute Manager* (incidentally, we are co-authors of the book,

Helping People Win at Work). "When you consider them separately, they're nice enough. But it's when you assemble them in just the right order, as a grouping they make the most sense. And they just don't work as well when you try to fit them in any other way.

"The real genius of them is in how each one creates a safe, supportive environment for the next one—if you move from largest to smallest. If you move from smallest to largest, each one gives the next one meaning and context. Values are like that too.

"People ask me what companies practice rank ordering of their values," he goes on to say. "My answer is easy: Only the best ones. Nordstrom. Southwest Airlines. Disney. Wegmans. And, of course, WD-40 Company."

In a values-run company culture, the *pleasure in the job*, as Aristotle put it, comes when our tribe members come to work every day feeling happy to be there, trusting their fellow tribe members, knowing that they will be supported in all they do, inside a circle of safety. They are proud of their work to bring to the world a product that makes a positive, lasting difference in the lives of their customers. They go home at night satisfied that their best talents continue to be invested in an effort to make the world a better place. And that they can count on the fact that the next day will bring more of the same: a working environment where they can trust, be trusted, celebrate and be celebrated. Come what may.

When people ask me to help them understand what makes the WD-40 Company culture so successful, I introduce them to this simple formula:

$$\text{Culture} = (\text{values} + \text{behavior}) \times \text{consistency}$$

All those variables and the result of a rewarding culture depend on a deep loyalty to the quality of our individual interactions and decision-making processes in service of our company and fellow tribe members. Other companies may create a list of feel-good values that are easily expressed on company walls, posters, and a page on their websites. And that's all well and good.

But we at WD-40 Company have learned that by creating a values set that truly resonates with authenticity and specificity and by placing them inside a hierarchical structure, we are unleashed to do the thing that prevails over all else—to create positive and lasting memories. Family by family. Household by household. All around the world.

Chapter 9
Leadership Lessons of Lockdown 2020

WE PURPOSE-DRIVEN business leaders and experts spend a significant portion of our lives traveling the world (at least in normal times), addressing groups of people with the hope that we might shift some perspectives, inspire new futures, open some questions that only the audience members can answer for themselves, or change a career or business trajectory for the better—even if only just a little. With the exception of a shared meal and posing for some grip-and-grins now and then, we don't often have much opportunity to really converse with the individuals in our audiences to learn if what we have to say makes any difference to them at all. Most of the time, outside of those we lead in our companies, we just don't really know what influence we have had.

For that reason, we especially welcome emails—or, even better, handwritten notes—from individuals who have heard what we offered. When it does happen, they typically start out by saying, "You probably don't remember me, but …" I received such a note just last week. And the writer was correct, I didn't remember him. But I'll never forget him now.

It's not so much because what I said helped him make a deeply satisfying career change that more closely aligned with his values. It's because of what he said happened one day on the way home from the hardware store.

As with most of us over the months of the Covid-19 lockdown, this young father had some time flexibility. He decided to use it by getting into bicycling again. Which required that he get his bike back into good working order. Which required that he clean his bike chain. Which required a trip to the store to pick up a can of WD-40 Multi-Use Product™.

He decided to bring along his 10-year-old daughter, who shruggingly accompanied him. And this is where we pick up his story:

"On the way home, I asked her, 'Do you know what we just bought?'

"'Some oil or something,' she said, while staring at the screen on her phone.

"'No, we just bought a memory.'

"When we got home, I asked her to help me clean the bike chain. I sprayed a rag with the WD-40 and told her to smell it. I then said, 'You will remember this moment forever. Every time you smell WD-40 from now on, you will remember this time we had together.'"

Considering that I am the chairman and CEO of WD-40 Company, I would understand it if you were beginning to think that I wrote this piece to do a commercial. But it could have just as easily been a roll of Gorilla Tape that he was talking about. And I would have still told this story.

Why? Because we're in the memories business. Yes, at WD-40 Company, we explicitly state this in our company's purpose: "We exist to create positive lasting memories in everything we do. We solve problems. We make things work smoothly. We create opportunities."

We elaborate on our commitment to memories in our second value: "We value creating positive lasting memories in all our relationships. As a result of our interactions with our tribe and stakeholders, we all will feel better at the end of the interaction than we did when we began; we will leave with a positive memory of it. Our stockholders should be proud to say they own our stock. Our customers should consider us a part of their business success. Consumers should be glad they bought our products, telling their friends about the quality and utility of our brands. Our company name and our many brands should become known as emblems of quality, performance and value. Our tribe members should consider each other valued friends and colleagues who share work, struggles, successes, life and laughter over the years. If we live these values, the result will be a higher degree of mutual trust and respect, if we successfully live these values."

But this is my challenge to you as a leader: Aren't we all in the memories business? Isn't this especially true when it comes to the way our people connect their talents, days, and careers with the company they work for?

Even more to the point: We're all in the business of creating *positive, lasting memories* that will be nourished well into the distant future by the way we touch our people, their families, and even future generations. This young father with his 10-year-old daughter had the foresight to understand that this was not just an annoying errand with an indifferent child in the passenger seat. He knew that if he framed this experience in just the right light, his daughter would not only remember this otherwise very ordinary experience, but she will likely tell her own children about "that time when," and hand them a piece of cloth so they could smell the same smell that evokes a loving, sentimental memory of her experience with her father. And her children will, in turn, do the same with their kids far into a future that we can't even begin to imagine today—removing the dirt and squeaks from toys yet to be invented.

In fact, it wouldn't surprise me in the slightest if this father had had the same experience with his own dad while working on a bike in the 1990s. Or something similar. Such a shared moment can have a permanent, positive bonding impact. Which brings us to where we find ourselves today.

What Will Your People Remember from the Lockdown of 2020?

Depending on where you are in the world, and where your people are located, the saga has a diversity of start dates. In the United States, for instance, most people point to March 16 when the national lockdown commenced. Others point to the troubling day of Friday, March 13th, when those who were traveling scrambled to airports in order to get home before that would become either complicated or impossible.

As for me, everything changed a couple of weeks beforehand. It was in late in February. I was, as usual, traveling. I was in a small town outside of Rome attending a conference for my company. At this point, we already knew that China was suffering. During that conference, Italy got hit. One-by-one, meetings all over the planet began to be cancelled. The effects of this mysterious and deadly contagion rolled around the globe like that big stone ball in the movie *Raiders of the Lost Ark*. I felt like Indiana Jones, running just barely ahead of it, working with our leaders to ensure all our facilities across 15 countries had action plans in place, and then get safely back to California, walk through my own front door and close it behind me by the time the calendar flipped to March 16.

At that point, the entire world community entered a chapter in the history of humanity that none of us have ever experienced before at such an epic scale, with an as-yet unknown outcome, and unforeseeable personal and economic implications. Everyone all over the world wondered "What do we do with this?" Business leaders around the globe asked themselves the same question. And we are still asking ourselves that question, as of this writing, doing our best to arrive at answers as things continually change.

One of the key components to the answers we can come up with—answers that are within our power to actually convert into outcomes—is the decision on how we will apply our leadership principles, values, and commitment to our respective cultural attributes to ensure that we serve our people so that they emerge from this experience whole, supported, and perhaps even transformed for the better, having had this shared experience.

When Employee Engagement Takes on a Whole New Meaning

Now would be the time when we would put all our long-cherished engagement drivers and cultural commitments to the test. The decisions and values-based choices we would make moving forward would create the memories for our people not only in the immediate fiscal year but for generations to come. What stories will they tell each other and their families about how WD-40 Company upheld its values?

You may remember in an earlier chapter that my own personal journey into the world and rewards of sincere commitment to employee engagement began in 1997—predictably—on a flight across the Pacific, from Los Angeles to Sydney. Up until that trip, my leadership style could be easily summed up this way: "Be brief, be bright, be gone." I was a just-get-it-done kind of leader, operating on the principle that if I kept moving fast, people would forget that I was really just a one-time traveling salesman from Australia.

But during that flight, I read these words by the Dalai Lama, which changed everything for me:

"Our prime purpose in this life is to help others. And if you can't help them, at least don't hurt them."

These words put me on a new leadership path, pursuing the foundation of a leadership master's degree program at the University of San Diego, where I was fortunate enough to have Ken Blanchard as my professor and mentor. All these years later, he still is.

As I progressed in my understanding of how to apply what I was learning, it became reflected by WD-40 Company's performance. When I started my role as CEO in 1997, WD-40 Company was primarily a domestic business serving a U.S. market. Our market cap was a mere $250 million. Respectable for our company at that time, but definitely modest. Worse, however, was that our overall employee engagement score was just shy of 50%.

As of 2020, over two decades into this adventure of transforming WD-40 Company into a truly global enterprise, with sales in 176 countries, our market cap is over $2.5 billion at the time of this writing. It's no coincidence that now our overall employee engagement score as of March 2020 is 93%. The one engagement indicator that I am especially proud of is: "I *love* to tell people I work for WD-40 Company," with 98% of our employees agreeing with that sentiment.

The results of WD-40 Company have been created over time based on our deep commitment to creating a tribal culture, where people feel that they belong, that they are connected to fellow tribe members, mutually invested in helping each other succeed. We pursue a culture where people believe that their leadership sincerely cares about their well-being, and they have a place to go to every day where they can do good and meaningful work, where they are happy to see people who are happy to see them as well. And at the end of the day, they go home feeling fulfilled for having done work that helps them express their own individual sense of purpose.

And then Covid-19 hit. And everyone went home. I feared the WD-40 Company circle of safety would be shattered into thousands of shards—one shard per home address. Suddenly, other than online video calls, there was no certainty when anyone would actually see anyone else again. In a new context of isolation and survival-level uncertainty, the WD-40 Company tribe needed care from their leaders with a new frame of reference into the future.

As it happened, just a few months prior, Simon Sinek had released his book *The Infinite Game*, in which he challenges readers to take on a larger mission than his famous *why*. Now he was talking about the Just Cause. Sinek states that a Just Cause is "a specific vision of a future state that does not yet exist; a future state so appealing that people are willing to make sacrifices in order to help advance toward that vision." The Just Cause, he writes, positions a company to prevail over the short-term challenges of quarterly performance demands, shifts in the marketplace, changing consumer needs or upheavals in global economic conditions. If there was ever a time to go through the exercise of identifying and articulating WD-40 Company's Just Cause, the Fall of 2019 would have been it. And we did, not knowing what was to come, or how valuable it would be to us just a few months later.

In addition to our purpose, and our values, we now have a Just Cause. It is this:

Make life better at work and at home.

As our tribe members' front doors clicked shut one by one all around the world, my role was to hold our Just Cause top of mind and continuously ask myself the same question I ask myself today, "What needs to be true for this day to be better for our tribe at work and at home?" (This question was inspired by the work of Rebecca Homkes, Ph.D, a consultant and lecturer at the London Business School.)

My main role is to keep them connected, nurture that tribal feeling of belonging and trust. Workplace experts are now reporting that the experience and experiment of grand-scale remote work is disenfranchising our cherished people. I can say with some humility that because of our 23 years' commitment to getting our culture of belonging right and authentic, our tribal network started out tight and intact, as was reflected in our engagement statistics. But I take nothing for granted, certainly not the feelings of the WD-40 Company tribe. My daily job—and privilege—is to serve them.

These are the leadership lessons I've learned along this journey ... so far. I hope you will be able to adapt them to your own Just Cause, as you navigate the turbulence, leading your organizations toward a brighter future.

Recognize That Employees Are on a Hero's Journey of Their Own

When your people finally return to your workplace, they will be coming back transformed for having gone through the experience of this pandemic. It takes special characteristics to be working "at home," living on the edge of uncertainty, without the in-person support of fellow tribe members. There's the adrenaline rush of unexpected possibilities; the thrill of the last-minute saves; the satisfaction of going it alone, even when the destination is unclear.

Every single level of Maslow's hierarchy of needs has been yanked out from each person, like a Jenga tower puzzle piece, causing levels of anxiety that few have experienced before. Add on top of that the isolation from each person's work tribe, the obliteration of the "circle of safety," the added stress of family members being on top of each other, lonely and bored children trying to learn from a computer screen, lack of exercise, unhealthy stress-management habits, the very real threat of the virus itself, and the constant stress of worrying about the uncontrollable.

It will take many years for behavioral science and health researchers from all disciplines to fully understand the long-term ramifications of this global isolation. And, to be candid, physical injury, violence and death are also playing out in many homes. There's substance abuse, child abuse and neglect, malnutrition, stress and anxiety-induced substance abuse. And there is no one from the outside to see.

And then there is the devastation by the coronavirus itself—the lives it will have taken, the families it will have harmed, and the loss of faith in many governmental and health systems.

This global calamity can be experienced as either a traumatic catastrophe or the makings of an epic adventure where your people will emerge stronger, wiser, braver, more resilient, and more confident for having overcome the huge challenges of this saga.

Those who prevail will emerge from this experience transformed. Exactly how the changes will manifest themselves remains a mystery as of this writing. But wise leaders will do well to bear in mind that the person they might have said, "Have a great weekend!" to on March 13 is not be the same person they will say, "Welcome back!" to when people return.

As leaders, we can't forget that our people have also had to envision and prepare for worst-case scenarios unlike anything they'd experienced in the past. They've learned new ways of coping, new ways of facing fear head on, new ways of finding the gifts in the midst of disaster.

They will be changing before your very eyes. Look closely and you might even be able to see it on a Zoom call. Reacquaint yourself with the people you used to know, and who have changed. Adjust your leadership approach accordingly.

Embrace the Learning Moment

As Indiana Jones said in *Raiders of the Lost Ark*, "I'm making this up as I go." If you have followed my writing over recent years, you know that even in the best of times, the Learning Moment is essential to creating a circle of safety in your workplace community where your people are free to try things (ideas, products, techniques, strategies) without fear of shame or reprisals should the experiment fail.

If there was ever a time when we're all learning as we go, it's now. What part of your business hasn't been touched by the pandemic of 2020? Our meetings are virtual (with at least one child, dog or cat photobombing the background), our systems have been retooled, our relationships with our vendors and customers have changed, our performance management systems have to be reimagined. We have to learn new tricks. And we're not always going to get them right. At least not the first time we try.

Our ways of doing our work in each company is part of our secret sauce. Our personal sack of hacks gives us a professional competitive edge. And now they're being tested as we learn how to work with each other over, say, Zoom.

Back in 1997, as I was transitioning into my CEO role at WD-40 Company, I still held the belief that the currency of power within the organization was the knowledge we each harbored and doled out in small bits only when it served our individual purposes. I believed that the more knowledge you had and controlled, the more power you also held and controlled.

But I realized through my new learning that the hoarding of knowledge was actually driven by fear. As much as we were fearful of losing our competitive edge as individual contributors, we were also afraid of not knowing something to the point of making a mistake. We were concerned that we would be ridiculed, humiliated, maybe even punished for any error that we might have made. As individuals, our personal standing was at stake. We felt our careers were at risk every time we shared or tried something new. When you come down to it, our sense of personal security hinged on every decision we made as to whether to share, experiment, expand, or learn.

As the CEO, I recognized that we needed a much different culture, a culture where the silos of knowledge would be transformed into fields of learning. In safe learning environments, there would be no shame associated with failure. In fact, there would be no failure at all.

Thus was born the concept of the Learning Moment: A positive or negative outcome of any situation that should be openly and freely shared to benefit all. The Learning Moment is an opportunity to grow from the experience of our colleagues, who are free to report back to us, "Wow, I just had a learning moment! Here is what it was and here is what I learned from it."

Replace Fear with Vision

Fear is a fundamental part of our nature—it's what our species has used to stay alive long enough over the eons to eventually result in, well, us.

Over hundreds of thousands of years, our brains evolved to fear the lion, to be very sensitive to environmental cues of threat. Dreaming about tomorrow's patch of savannah grass never saved the antelope. But knowing exactly where that pride of hungry lions was crouching in wait to strike surely saved the more quick-witted grazers. Antelopes and humanoids all got the survival gift of developing brains that are more interested in the worst-case scenario than the possibilities of a brighter future ahead. That's how we survived into the 21st century where we are now concerning ourselves with global supply chains, whether our truckers feel safe on the highways' rest stops, how easily we can source raw material from other countries when our main supplier is shut down, and how we explain our latest market performance to our investors.

There's no getting around it. We're all surrounded by figurative lions that we hadn't planned for last year. We didn't even have a clue they were lurking in the tall grass. These potential threats absorb a huge portion of our attention.

But that focus on current threats is not where tomorrow's greener pastures can be found. As leaders we owe it to our tribe to hold the vision of a better day safe for them. And to make that vision accessible all the time. We have to paint the picture of where we're going, even as we lead through where we are today.

It's been said, "Where there is no vision, the people perish." Your tribe members may be working hard to avoid the current set of survival threats, but they still need to know what the vision is. What is the dream that will make this all worthwhile at the end? Managers might keep their people focused on the short-term goals for the next period or payday. But you're the leader. It's up to you to paint a more vivid picture of the larger landscape of possibility.

In his book *Emergence: 7 Steps for Radical Life Change*, Derek Rydall wrote: "True vision is part of … what Plato called the realm of perfect prototypes or ideal forms. It comes from a place beyond the mind, beyond, time, beyond space, and beyond experience."

Rydall describes an ant determinedly making its way to a very large potato chip, a chip that looms so large it obscures the ant's ability to see an entire universe of possibilities beyond the chip. The manager is like that ant sometimes, concerned with the chip. You, the organizational leader, have the higher perspective of being able to see what lies beyond the chip. An entire universe of future possibilities, once that chip is dealt with.

Hold the vision of the larger array of life's possibilities and business growth beyond the current state of affairs. Show the evidence for hope of a new day. That will be the inspiration that drives your tribe's collective energy and commitment into the future. Then your people will become your partners in manifesting the vision that you see together.

Communicate with Your Tribe More Than You Ever Have; Communicate More Than You Think You Need To

Many leaders might naturally assume that I'm advising readers to communicate more *to* their tribe members. That might be true but only in part. I believe that we should speak *with* our tribe members, making communication truly a two-way street in which everyone has the chance to hear and, even more importantly, be heard.

My tribe members are crucial to the health of WD-40 Company and our shared future together. There is no way I could successfully do what I do without the companionship and the mutual support the WD-40 Company tribe members share with each other. I feel humbly grateful to be among this wonderful community of selfless, innovative, committed individuals.

As I am the CEO, they naturally do want to hear from me—and all our leaders—about company news and the strategies that are being developed. They welcome even the hard news and difficult decisions, because they need to hear the truth, as frequently as is possible and relevant. I also make a point of sending out handwritten notecards every day to singularly acknowledge individuals within the tribe, and even to external relationships I deeply value. I hear it means a lot to people to receive these notes. But the time it takes me to thoughtfully think about how grateful I am for our friendship and their contributions to this journey we're all on gives me the time to fully feel that very real gratitude that I have for being in this role with these wonderful people.

Likewise, it's very important for our tribe members to be able to speak to each other and to me! We're well past the time when the Covid-related work-from-home workstyle is a novelty. For many, loneliness and isolation are setting in. We must find other ways to use communication to keep our cultural fabric intact.

Encourage your people to communicate directly with you. And respond to them personally, with individualized messages to prove that you have read their message and that it is, indeed, you who are responding. Encourage your tribe members to communicate with each other as much as possible, whenever they want to. Keep an online virtual meeting room open, for instance, for people to simply drop in and break up the day with a "water cooler" chat with each other. Keep your cultural values, company purpose or Just Cause conversations alive by asking your tribe members to tell stories of how the Just Cause is being served, even in work-from-home situations.

Vibrant, constant communication can be achieved. By the time everyone returns to work for real, they will be re-engaging with friends, not strangers they used to know.

Let Empathy Lead the Way

Empathy is a difficult emotional concept for many leaders, especially during a time in our history when it's all we can do to keep ourselves composed and focused on the challenges before us. For many of us, *empathy* evokes rather squishy emotional boundaries where we're being asked to take on the full weight of another person's suffering. Actually, that is the sense of *sympathy*, where we actually feel as badly as the other person who is suffering. Empathy is understanding how another person is feeling, validating that their experience is real. Sympathy is very expensive emotionally and not productive. Empathy is powerful and engaging.

When I talk about empathy, it's almost always in the context of contrasting it with *ego*, which will get you into trouble. *Empathy*, no matter how you define it, always involves caring about others, fully understanding whatever it is that they're suffering through. *Ego,* by contrast, is focusing attention on oneself. When you make leadership all about you, you shut out the possibilities and good will of others who would otherwise be well-positioned to help you achieve your most important objectives.

In times of intensity, the ego state is more likely to emerge. Leaders are more inclined to seize control—or at least try to. It's based on some level of insecurity, reacting to outside pressures. Impatience. Fear. All these impulses are perfectly understandable. We're all human. But they cause disasters that are perfectly avoidable.

Commitment to empathy is the tempering stance that causes leaders to pause, listen, and consider other peoples' perspectives and ideas, even in those hair-on-fire moments when speed to action seems to be the only course. That pause to listen to another's perspective could be all that's required to find a better solution to the emergency.

The ability to feel other peoples' feelings and see things from other peoples' perspectives is the cornerstone of servant leadership. When you bring that leadership philosophy into your company culture—even a virtual one—you lay down a foundation of trust. And on that foundation, your people experience what it's like to be respectfully listened to and actually heard. And from there they feel free to contribute innovation, creativity and discretionary effort. They will be more likely to bring Learning Moments to the table, instead of hiding them.

Empathy is about having a heart of gold and a backbone of steel. It's about being tough-minded and tender-hearted. Empathy is also about loving someone enough to have that hard conversation, the conversation that can save a life, a career, or a global company.

It's also about forgiving everyone for simply being human. We're seeing each other's humanity more than ever these days, simply via Zoom or Webex. We can tell just by looking over our coworkers' shoulder whether they made their bed that morning. We see what brand of cereal their children like. On one live webinar, the speaker's cat walked into view and proceeded to throw up in front of a global audience.

Which conveniently brings me to the next leadership lesson:

Don't Try to Control Things
Beyond Your Reach

There are some things we just can't know about. We don't know what the future will bring. True, you can close the door on your cat, which might have been a good idea in the above example. But if you truly can't change a situation, a circumstance, a condition … let it go.

None of us can say for sure that we know precisely where we're going within the foreseeable future. If you were to talk to your December 2019 self from your 2020 perspective, you would likely bust out laughing at your projections. As Westley said in *The Princess Bride*, "Get used to disappointment."

As a collective world of businesses, the best we can say for the moment—at least in terms of strategic planning—is "We're about direction, not destination." You can control the general compass settings of your strategic initiatives. You can adjust course as you travel, to keep yourself heading in the general direction of your objectives. But you still have no solid control over your final destination (although it would be nice to get as close to it as possible), nor your time of arrival.

These current conditions have never confronted us before. But now that they have, the only expectation we can be relatively certain of is that they will visit us again. Maybe in not quite the same form or magnitude of impact. Or maybe it will be even worse (assuming that's possible). Maybe we'll be prepared next time for the resulting impact on our business. Or maybe it will be an entirely different scenario, one that yet again we didn't see coming.

(This year, a popular self-help writer wrote about her life of struggles from the perspective of having prevailed over a series of unforeseen disasters, all leading up to the lockdown. Her book is entitled, *Didn't See That Coming*. Just as she completed the manuscript with that sigh of satisfaction of a massive project accomplished, and she was about to ship the file to her publisher, her husband of 18 years told her that he wanted a divorce. Their "successful" marriage had been part of her brand. She didn't see that coming, either. And then her fanbase roundly—and loudly—criticized her for the perception that she was monetizing her breakup with the publication of the book. She didn't see that coming either. It just never stops coming, does it?)

The best thing we can do is come to terms with uncertainty, which a friend once defined for me as the way we regard a series of future events that may or may not happen. Almost all of the data and information that we were so confident about in 2019 is useless to us now. While not all our inputs are irrelevant at this point, we have the added need to determine what remains a legitimate assumption or projection. And what should simply be thrown over in the dust bin of "That was then, this is now."

When the world started shutting down, we launched a process company-wide called Stabilize/Secure, Reset, and Thrive (also created by Rebecca Homkes). The first stage, **Stabilize/Secure**, had us all reviewing our circumstances, resources, and motivation, to decide how we would prevail under constantly shifting conditions. We determined to simply get the basics right, to be responsive to all incoming expressions of concerns from all our partners and tribe members, and to set up clear communications to our tribe—relying on our already healthy relationship with them and the trust that was embedded in our culture—and to steepen our learning velocity. We had no time to waste, learning what we needed to learn to survive in these constantly shifting conditions.

Next was **Reset**. Readers of *Who Moved My Cheese?* will recognize the principle that when facts change, we have to change our beliefs and approaches to our desired outcome accordingly. Our old beliefs just aren't valid anymore. So what would be the new belief set? What is the new definition of success? And what is the new path—or at least direction—toward that objective? And, finally, how agile are we to make a new pivot when conditions change yet again? And then again? And then again?

Finally, **Thrive**: What are our new competitive advantages in the changed business landscape? Where are the opportunities that have not been revealed under the changed conditions? What do we need to do differently? To do better? To do unexpectedly?

What's within your reach to control today may be beyond your reach tomorrow. As long as you're headed in the same general direction of your vision, and your people can see the rationale and logic behind your initiatives, you're operating within your scope of reach. And that's the best you can ask of yourself. For the time being.

Be Clear About Intent

Even with such ambiguity, everything you say and do, every decision you affirmatively make and announce, should reasonably, logically, and transparently be able to fit into the larger picture that is understandable by your constituents. How do you accomplish this degree of certitude in an environment where the best you can aim for is a general direction, not a specific destination? You distill your decisions through the filters of your values, your purpose, and your Just Cause.

These parameters are our boundaries, our guard rails to keep us on the road and headed in our desired direction. When we are able to say to all our shareholders, "We will not move outside of our values just because we're in this situation," we are able to extend the message that our intent is to always be the community, the company, that stands by what we believe in the most.

Studies have shown that employee populations are more likely to accept and even activate unpopular decisions from the top if their leadership takes the time to intentionally explain the rationale for those decisions. Even if the employees still don't agree with the ultimate direction of the initiatives, they are more likely to support them because their leaders demonstrate the respect necessary to engage them in understanding the rationale behind the decisions.

Inviting collaboration in this way is especially valuable during these chaotic times. You want your people to be creative, collaborative, reliable, cooperative, innovative. For them to be all those things, they need one main emotional condition: A strong feeling of that circle of safety that normally comes from the daily face-to-face interaction in a trusting environment. As so much is being done virtually now, the *intention* of being intentional must be even more, well, intentional.

There is a feeling of safety and comfort in knowing that whatever surprises are sprung and swung our way, each decision is made with the utmost of care and respect for the entire community. To achieve that experience among your people, you must slow down, be explicit in your thinking process, and show them how your decision stays within the guiding beacons that were established long before chaos hit the fan.

Resist the Temptation to Micromanage

In stressful situations, people tend to want to micromanage more than they had in more normal times. If you're intentional with your boundaries as we discussed above, you are better equipped to resist the emotional compulsion to "take the wheel."

One of the most inspiring presentations I've ever seen is a speech by U.S. Air Force (retired) Colonel Nicole Malachowski, who, along with being a combat veteran, flew with the precision Thunderbirds Air Demonstration Squadron. You have probably seen pictures of the formation of these jets in air. It looks like they're flying wing-tip to wing-tip. Fast. All the planning must be done first on the ground. Once they're in motion, the order is to "fly loose," with the hand lightly touching the stick regardless of whatever effects the turbulence is having on the jet.

In the presentation, she introduces the term, "pilot-induced oscillation," which isn't a good thing. "Big movements, bigger corrections," she says. "That's not how you nurture change." In the wing-tip to wing-tip formation's collective agreement among all the Thunderbirds pilots, pilot-induced oscillation would produce a catastrophe as each jet collides with the next because one pilot reacted independently and out of agreement from the plans established beforehand.

"Not only does it make for a really ugly air show," she said, "It's also extraordinarily unsafe and makes the change even worse."

In these current conditions, we're flying in turbulence. Wing-tip to wing-tip. There is just no getting around it. As a team, make your plans and processes "on the ground," where it's still safe and theoretical, where nothing will crash. And then let your team fly the plan. They are your experts, and they are airborne. Trust them.

Practice Pragmatic Optimism

You've hopefully relinquished your grip on the idea that you can dictate to the future exactly what you want and when you want it. You and your team are now happy to just stick with the idea of "general direction" for the time being, until conditions stabilize (notice I didn't say *normalize*). Everyone has become realists given the undeniable circumstances. But it's your job to keep them from becoming pessimists. This is how you achieve a cultural climate of "pragmatic optimism," without offering up your company's version of unicorns and rainbows.

Your people want to believe in a future worth working toward. But very recent memory (even current conditions) tells a different story: Dashed expectations that seemed very realistic just last year (assuming you're reading this in 2020); missed goals and projections at work; cancelled weddings, and even cancelled funerals. Jobs have been lost. Many small businesses shut down forever.

So what's pragmatic optimism? I call it "optimism with a foundation." First let's look at optimism. Martin Seligman, considered the founder of the positive psychology movement, speaks of optimism as a life philosophy that whatever the current conditions might be, they're not permanent. They're also not personal. And they're not likely to be within anyone's power to change somehow. No, COVID-19 is not likely to be within any one person's ability to eliminate from the planet forever. But your response to it and how it affects the way you live your life on a day-to-day basis is at least somewhat within your grasp. It's within everyone's power to decide how to govern its influence in their lives based on their behavior choices. That point of view is the beginning of optimism.

As business leaders we can know what our variables are. We know what our resources are, what our Just Cause is, what our talent bench strength is. From there we can start building up the detailed plans for the changes we need to make to create the future we all imagine inside our circle of safety.

Plan for the Next Iteration

Even if you don't know what the next iteration is, what needs to be true for it to be perfect? You and your tribe might still have some of that time flexibility to prepare for elements necessary to create the ideal next iteration.

WD-40 Company has been here before. In the market crash of 2008-2009, when the bottom fell out of business worldwide, most large global companies reduced their exposure by shrinking their employee population through early retirement, furloughs and lay-offs. We went the other way at WD-40 Company.

I was inspired by American baseball (which I knew a little bit about because Australia has a similar game that I grew up with). One day it hit me, "Great players don't keep their form by sitting on the bench." If we were to have our top talent—our entire tribe, really—be in top form and ready to take on the next wave of market upswing and the opportunities that come with it—let's raise the professional development bar. So while other companies were shedding their talent, we were building up our talent. And by the time that economic period had run its course, we were ready to take action with a whole new collection of updated skills throughout the entire organization. We made excellent use of that time.

Circumstances are different now, though. Back then, we weren't forced to physically separate and isolate. We're doing more online training now, obviously. But more to the point, we're learning to pivot around fear and keep our future top of mind. We will be ready for the next iteration of the entire world, when it comes around again.

We will also know that with each new iteration, we must remind ourselves, "This too shall pass." The good and the bad. Fly loose. The tribe will prevail.

Honor Your Own Hero's Journey

In a cascading series of events around the world, we all left our offices for the last time and went home. Generally speaking, our expectation was perhaps a four- to six-week event, "just to flatten the curve." And then the extension lengthened by two more weeks, then a month, etc. You know the rest. You're likely to be still living it now in some fashion or another.

I may be the CEO and Chairman of a company that is so essential to everyday life that a young father will take his 10-year-old daughter on a hardware store errand to acquire a can that will improve their lives at home. But I'm also an employee of WD-40 Company, just like all my fellow tribe members. And as such, I am home with my wife Maria and my, by now, world-famous black Lab-shepherd-Great Dane rescue mix, Max the Wonder Dog.

I have my daily routines, which includes exercise (although maybe not as daily as I'd like it to be). I have my home office, which now has a place specifically set up for my Zoom calls and live webinars. I have my books. I have my calls with the leadership teams, the board, and the investors. And I have my own Hero's Journey that I have embarked on.

Like all my fellow tribe members, I am learning about life in new ways. My three big discoveries so far:

1. **Free Flow Fridays.** On this day Maria and I commit to taking the week's pent-up tensions and frustrations and just, phew, let it all go.

2. **To never lose sight of the joy and privilege of my life's purpose as it is expressed through my work.** As we've already discussed, Aristotle said, "Pleasure in the job puts perfection in the work." I am serving my life's purpose as CEO of WD-40 Company. It is my pleasure. And it's also my responsibility to role model that pleasure to my tribe so their spirits will stay aloft as well.

3. **And, forgive myself (and others) for being human.** We're all learning new ways of doing things, about being tribe members, about running a global company, about responding to mixed signals and constant changes in policies state by state, nation by nation, market by market.

New learnings mean new opportunities to try new ways. Which, in turn, means new opportunities to experiment.

Which means new Learning Moments to bring to the tribe!

I value every opportunity to contribute my own Learning Moments to the learning of others.

How Will You Use the Memories of 2020?

Catastrophic events have shifted the known business world on its axis throughout human history. Each event, from Mount Vesuvius swamping lava over the small businesses in Pompeii in 79 AD, through the devastations of the U.S. Civil War in the 1860s, through the Great Depression through the obliteration of modern European cities during WW 2, to the massive fires in my homeland in Australia, ordinary citizens watched their worlds turn upside down and crumble. No doubt their survival instinct was encouraged with the thought, "It can't possibly get any worse than this." Ah. But history shows us it can. Just in different, unpredictable ways.

I think it's safe to say that the year 2020 has presented the most tumultuous challenges that our current generation of corporate leadership has ever seen. Not just one. But many. We can only hope it won't get any worse than this. But history, as we have already seen, would tell us otherwise. And they seem to be speeding up in frequency, the intervals shortening. To be realistic, we are likely to still be in the leadership seat when the next hammer drops.

In every classic Hero's Journey, the hero acquires tools, skills, lessons along the way to bring back to the tribe. In this case, I hope you will have picked up the lessons, skills, and tools necessary to have built a resilient culture of vision-inspired tribe members who trust and support one another, who create that essential circle of safety that will enable them to not only watch out for the threats but also to spot the opportunities.

As for me? Yes, I'm still a one-time traveling salesman from Australia. But now, in my own Hero's Journey, I hope I have acquired the skills and tools to teach and inspire other leaders how to create a culture that treats people with respect and dignity, a place of learning and sharing, that survives in bad times, thrives in great times, and has employee engagement that is admired around the world, with an extremely successful financial track record to prove Aristotle's axiom throughout the organization.

Will this time we're in right now be just the latest in the historic series of catastrophic episodes that shake humanity awake from the complacency of normalcy bias, only to go back to sleep again?

Or will it be the ultimate Learning Moment that will equip you and your tribe to advance, prepared to take on the next one, making epic memories along the way to inspire and teach future generations? You're the leader. You are the one who must decide.

Chapter 10

Confidential to CEOs:
Grateful for the Gift of Belonging

THIS IS THE time of year when, all over the world, we traditionally pause to reflect on the past months to review what we learned and what we're grateful for. This year, however, is a little different. Wouldn't you say? If we were to run an imaginary video of the scenes from the year through our mind, we'd see a succession of images we couldn't have imagined this time in 2019. Depending on where you are in the world, those images might include devastating wildfires, crowds of black umbrellas shielding the identities of protestors and rioters, small businesses ablaze, Zoom funerals, football stadiums with digitized fans, families figuring out their dwindling finances as one spouse's career is derailed, children trying their best to learn through a laptop screen while missing their friends. Tent cities of homeless and utterly desolate urban streets. Water cannons assaulting peaceful demonstrations in modern cities.

Where is the gratitude to be found amongst this rubble?

In this context, I was asked to write about what I am grateful for as a CEO in 2020. While I've been mulling this assignment over, several things happened to me that have helped me enrich my thinking. And this is what I'd like to share with you now.

Over the Thanksgiving weekend, a friend sent me a copy of the speech Abraham Lincoln gave when he inaugurated the first official Thanksgiving

Day in 1863, only halfway through the terrible Civil War, whose outcome was still unknown. How in the midst of bloodshed, devastation, ruined crops and cities, loss and tragedy could any leader proclaim any kind of Thanksgiving without sounding well, out of touch and tone deaf? He listed all the ways the United States was thriving even as the war was raging in a dense fog of uncertainty.

What struck me about all those ways? They told the story of industrious men and women using their skills, talents, and energies, working together with a shared vision of the future driving them forward, even when they were surrounded by the horrors of real and present devastation. Their shared vision of their country—be it unified or split in two, they would have to wait another 18 months to learn that outcome—was so compelling that they continued leaning into their labors to keep building and growing. Despite the immediate evidence all around them that told them that hope might be a fool's errand.

Work. How people express themselves through what they do for a living, together, evokes a greatness, a resilience, an expression of hope for the future, that brings a kind of human joy that's within reach no matter what the external circumstances might be. And then my mind's video player reminded me of images from this past year of Italian apartment building tenants singing soaring traditional songs up and down their air shafts. They might not have known each other in real life (or IRL, as we would all start saying in our newly virtual world), but they knew the same songs, they knew their parts in the harmonies. And they knew when to start banging their pots and pans at the point where percussion is traditionally called for.

Then I thought of those Zoom events when Nashville studio musicians and orchestra musicians would give free concerts. Each player or singer alone at home, performing into a computer that would feed each part into a distant server. Each participant contributing their profession, their work, from their heart, for free, to lift the spirits of the sequestered globe.

Then, naturally, the front-line health care workers. The truck drivers. The personal protection equipment manufacturers. All those distilleries that converted their plants to become hand sanitizer bottlers. The teachers who, on a dime, changed their instruction methods to pour hope and knowledge into a single monitor alone in a school room, which would then distribute it to hundreds of children throughout the country. As best they could. We were all figuring it out and beginning to see a light at the end of the tunnel.

And then the second thing happened. At least here in the United States. The presidential election, which remains highly contested even today, more than a month after the ballots were due in from coast to coast. Here in the United States, and throughout the rest of the world, we're watching the upheaval. And there's only one thing we know for sure at the moment: The conflict is turning families and friends from each other. Even the word "unity," spoken with the best of intentions, triggers outrage amongst the factions.

Here is Where It Gets Good in a Terrible Time

It was suggested to me that in my role as a CEO I craft a message to the WD-40 Company tribe members reminding them that we're all in this together; that even in the face of social strife, we should and must remember kindness and acceptance. That seems to be an obviously good idea, but something wasn't sitting right with the message. It just wasn't flowing. The tone was wrong. But I couldn't put my finger on it.

Then someone asked me the question that changed everything for me: "Have you seen evidence that your tribe is unraveling? Are people treating each other unkindly, in such a way that they need to actually hear an admonishment from you?"

Uhm. Come to think of it, actually, no. What I had witnessed over the previous year was something to celebrate, not admonish. I saw WD-40 Company tribe members pour their best efforts, ideas, flexibility and collaboration not only into their work but also into each other. This was a time for celebration, not for stern reminders of who we are. Every day WD-40 Company tribe members are showing me who they are and reminding me of who *I* can be when I bring my best to our shared vision of a better world, both at work and at home.

Here is a Small Piece of What I Wrote to My Tribe

My gratitude for my fellow WD-40 Company tribe members goes beyond anything I can adequately put into words. But I thought I would at least give it a go right here and now:

All throughout the world—especially where our tribe members live and work—there have been so many threats to our community fabric. Covid. Politics. Societal strife that has caused so many of us to question who we have become—as individuals and as a society. We have had to take good long looks in the mirror. Our relationships with the people we love have had to withstand stresses and strains we couldn't have even imagined last year. And, let's face it, we miss our tribe members. I know I certainly do. Every time I have had to go to our tepee, and walk the empty halls, passing by empty spaces that normally bustle with your energy, my loneliness for everyone sometimes feels so tangible I can practically wrap my hands around it.

And yet. I'm so proud of us all. Even as we each experience our own individual hero's journey that causes us to face new frontiers of private grief, fear, uncertainty, we have worked together as a tribe

- so seamlessly,
- so lovingly,
- so supportively,
- so acceptingly,
- so creatively
- so generously,

that no matter what our individual differences with each other might be, we are knitted together as a tribe in such a way that I don't think any of us will ever forget this time. We will look back on this period as the time when we showed the world who we are at our very hearts—to ourselves, to each other, to our partners, our families and our customers …

As we're entering the close of one year (and not a moment too soon, I might add), and looking forward to fresh promises of 2021, it gives me great joy to know we're going forward together as a tribe of shared mission, values, and mission for a better world at home and at work.

The Meaning of Belonging

You might be thinking to yourself, "Okay, right about now, he's going to say something about Viktor Frankl's *Man's Search for Meaning.*" Well, right about now, I will not disappoint you. Most people know about the first half of his book, where he details the horrors of life in Nazi concentration camps and discovers that when a prisoner is able to find meaning in the individual moments—no matter the suffering—he or she is more likely to survive the unspeakable deprivations. It's in the second half of the book, where he expands on *logotherapy*, that explains, from a psychologist's point of view, exactly what is behind the discoveries of the first half of the book. He writes

> … We have shown that the meaning of life always changes, but that it never ceases to be. According to logotherapy, we can discover this meaning in life in three different ways: (1) by creating a work or doing a deed; (2) by experiencing something or encountering someone; and (3) by the attitude we take toward unavoidable suffering.

Have we all not seen examples of all three of these ways in action, especially inside the work setting? In her weirdly prescient article from last year, "Why Corporate Culture, Values and Vision Will Save Society in 2020," author and employee engagement expert Martha Finney wrote: "Politicians and pundits will be spending the next year telling us why we should hate each other. But the business world is giving us everyday reasons why we can all love each other."

The workplace gives us a locus for labor, for resilience, and ultimately for a love of each other. The workplace gives us meaning.

We expected the political divisiveness that Martha wrote about. But we sure didn't expect *all this.* And yet, day after day, I have seen examples of my tribe members pulling together, loving each other, supporting each other, bringing out the best in each other, covering for each other when we just couldn't bring our best to the tribe. We fed and protected each other, just as a tribe does, according to Simon Sinek's definition of tribe.

That is what we do. That is what will see us through. That is what makes me so proud to be a member of my particular tribe. I concluded my message to my tribe with the invitation to send me stories of when they were most grateful to be a WD-40 Company tribe member in 2020. It's only been a couple of weeks, and I've already received upwards of 75 responses from people all over the world expressing their gratitude for belonging to the WD-40 Company tribe.

I would like to extend the same invitation to you and yours. How does this opportunity of belonging show up in your company? No matter what the external circumstances might be surrounding your business and challenging the resources of your people, there is a kind of meaningful peace that can come as everyone uses their work life to express a greater love for each other through their shared vision for a better time and world.

Send out the invitation to your people. See what comes back to you. And then tell me how it made you feel.

It would mean a lot to me.

Chapter 11
Nerves Of Real

IN CHAPTER 9, I introduced you to Col. Nicole Malachowski (USAF, retired), the first female fighter pilot in the Thunderbirds. She inspires the principle to "fly loose," advising us leaders to resist the urge to micromanage when conditions start getting, shall we say, "off plan." In her training and speeches, she points out that when flying in tight formation, coordinating six jets flying wing tip to wing tip at 500 miles per hour, there's no room for improvisation. Each pilot is expected to fly exactly according to plan with a light touch on the controls. Any rogue reaction by one pilot to an impulse becomes an overreaction by all the pilots, which then produces what she calls "pilot-induced oscillation." And then, as she puts it in exquisite, tragic understatement, that makes for an "ugly" performance.

Since that post was published, I have dived even further into my own thinking on this subject—an opportunity that coincided with the release of WD-40 Company's year-end earnings report for 2020. And I've come to appreciate in a fresh way something that we all know intellectually. But it's only when it gets really real that we fully grasp the enormity of this particular principle: The real power is in the planning on the ground long before the pilots take to the air. It's not just the allegiance to the wing-tip-wing-tip plan that matters. It's the quality of plan itself. That can only be done well in advance.

Whether it's a jaw-dropping exhibition of precision flying by the world's best pilots, or enviable news to corporate investors, the performance that makes spectators marvel—even exhale with "wow! That was close!"—starts not only with an excellent plan created in advance. It also comes from our commitment to being loyal to that plan—also in advance.

And that's what you have to be faithful to once everyone has committed to taking flight with you. We can't lose sight of the fact that when our tribe members agree to join our companies, they've strapped their lives and careers into very powerful jets, revving to take off. And they're counting on us to get the plan right. Because at that point they're all in. And they're counting on you, as the leader, to be all in too.

In the case of WD-40 Company, our commitment is to the culture. That's the plan around which everything else is determined.

One of my board members said to me this week, "It's in tough times like this when character is really tested." I responded: "It's in tough times like this when *our culture* is really tested. This year was not the outcome of any miraculous thing we did. It was the outcome of our commitment to the consistency of our culture, sustaining it based on the values and behavior we identified as core to the WD-40 Company experience years ago."

It's fashionable these days to speak of resilience—especially in the context of rebounding from hard times and hard knocks. But I think that resilience starts with *adherence*, our adherence to the promises we made to ourselves and each other when everyone is safely on the ground. Because when things start getting real, they will get really real. While outsiders may witness a spectacular performance and a safe landing at the end, we insiders, we tribe members, know what really went into the adventure—our promise to keep our promise to each other.

The Promise Behind the Plan

If you're new to the leadership thinking behind WD-40 Company, you have probably noticed my use of the word *tribe* when referring to our community. For quick reference, I define *tribe* as a group of people **who have come together to protect and feed each other.** Holding top of all our minds that we are tribe members who protect and feed each other helps us sustain our values—the very first of which is "do the right thing."

As the CEO, watching the country-by-country closing down of the planet back in March, what was top of my mind was the safety and well-being of all our tribe members. What did "do the right thing" mean when it came to the decisions we made to make sure our tribe members were protected and fed? I recognized that every one of our tribe members were living out their own individual stories of fear and anxiety, given their own particular family situation—and the stories of their friends losing their jobs and their favorite neighborhood restaurants and businesses going under. I was determined to give them that circle of safety that the tribe model provides, so that at least one aspect of their lives could be secure and dependable.

My own personal purpose echoes a message I once read by the Dalai Lama: "My purpose in life is to make people happy. If I can't make them happy, I at least won't hurt them."

WD-40 Company tribe members—and their well-being—were on my mind from the second I woke up in the morning (as a global CEO, "morning" became a hypothetical concept at best). And they were the on my mind as I got ready for bed at the end of each day. They were strapped into their lives, their jets propelled by their WD-40 Company careers. And it was my job to make sure they landed safely.

We needed a plan we could plan on. Happily, it was the plan we had created while everyone was safely on the ground—before March 13, 2020.

The Plan Behind the Promise

Well before the great global shutdown, we had created our strategic drivers that have been guiding us and helping set our objectives and must-win battles for 2020:

> **Grow WD-40 Multi-Use Product™.** Maximize the product line through geographic expansion, increased market penetration and development of new and unique delivery systems. More places. More people. More uses. More frequently.

Grow WD-40 Specialist product line. Leverage the WD-40 Specialist line to create growth through continued geographic expansion, as well as by developing new products and product categories within identified platforms.

Broaden product and revenue base. Leverage the recognized strengths of WD-40 Company to derive revenue from existing brands, as well as from new sources and products.

Attract, develop, and retain outstanding tribe members. Succeed as a tribe while excelling as individuals.

Operational excellence. Continue to cultivate operational excellence by optimizing resources, systems and processes, as well as applying rigorous commitment to quality assurance, regulatory compliance, and intellectual property protection.

Those strategic initiatives were identified and developed as our 2020 "flight plan" before the world turned upside down. Were they equally relevant to our tribe's well-being April 1 as they had been March 1? After careful consideration of the changing variables, we decided, "Yes they were." And so, our jets took to the air.

True, there had to be some retooling of our day-to-day processes (I mean, really, who knew online video meetings would become such a thing? And on the few occasions when I must go to our headquarters, the echoing, lonely emptiness of its hallways is palpable). We did things differently. But our goals never changed.

And I celebrate all our tribe members for our 2020 results. Net sales were up in the fourth quarter of 2020 compared to 2019. And, with the exception of a few areas in the global where DIY isn't a cultural attribute, we discovered a new consumer niche, a phrase coined beautifully by Tricia Tanton, our Canadian general manager, "isolation renovation." Additionally, a benefit from an initiative we started four years ago took unexpected shape in an unforeseen, accelerated way: Because we had decided to invest in raising our digital IQ and e-commerce competence very early, we were ready to serve our customers as they made a massive shift to buying online.

But, even more compellingly for me personally, is that we did the right thing by our tribe members. We protected them. And we fed them (or more to the point, we ran our business in such a way that they could continue to feed themselves, which is even better). In the 23 years I have been the CEO of WD-40 Company, we have never had to lay anyone off due to financial or marketplace reversal of fortunes. And that remains true today. The tribe is intact. The formation is wingtip-to-wingtip and we're flying fast.

We had developed our plan on the ground, before all jets took off, fully trusting the commitment of the leadership to the tribe. We are going places and we are landing safely.

This makes for a very beautiful performance.

Chapter 12

Using Virtual Tools to
Keep Our Culture Real

HERE AT WD-40 Company, we have a ritual that is very precious to me. It's a ritual of bonding, of hope, of release, of vulnerability and trust. And it goes this way:

About three times a year, different senior leadership groups come to San Diego from all over the world for their annual gathering. The ones who were here the year before know what to expect. The newcomers are transformed in ways they could never anticipate. Right before the first dinner, once we've all assembled, we make our way to a bonfire and receive our instructions. On small pieces of paper that are passed around, we're told to write one thing that we want to let go of and throw it into the fire. Those who want to are welcome to declare that thing aloud for the group to hear, for the San Diego night sky to hear, for the universe to hear.

As a tribe, we hear of cancer, of a wide variety of fears, angers, resentments, desires—personal, business, career concerns. We also have personal successes and joys that we want to celebrate by sending bonfire sparks up to the sky. We trust each other enough to reveal our paper's contents, and then we release that paper to the flames. It's a tribal ritual of letting go—of both the fears and the successes. And then we make our way to dinner as an entirely different, bonded tribe of hearts and hopes.

That ritual was put on pause one day in March 2020 as one by one we each went home from work and stayed there.

Like just about everyone else on the planet, we turned our faces toward our computer screens and smiled and waved at the familiar faces looking back at us. Meetings went virtual. We observed repeatedly what a break it is to have the world networked the way it is at such a time when work from home was the only way. Business got done—maybe in fits and starts at first. But we figured it out. And as global community we laughed at the mishaps that come with inside looks into everyone's personal life. Oh well.

But I felt our tribal equity draining away. At WD-40 Company, we're a tribe based on belonging, shared experiences, safe in collaborating and learning—even safe in failing. Without the day-to-day experience of each other, the void that was left behind became a hollow through which I worried we'd lose the spark that makes us ... us.

I know I'm not alone among corporate leaders in worrying about this. What about that intangible culture that we as a collection of dedicated leaders have invested years—if not decades—in intentionally developing? How do we keep our corporate cultures distinct and alive when everyone's closest coworker is behind a screen and a keyboard perhaps thousands of miles away? Where is the bonfire? Where is the spontaneous reveal of dreams, anxieties, hopes?

I'm discovering that online video services have a role in this new alchemy of culture nourishment. They've become more than scheduled meetings ticking off agenda items. They are opportunities for us to show each other our new babies. To laugh at the shared experience of meeting tight deadlines. To make new friends of colleagues we might have only known before by their company role. To learn new ways of doing life better.

And much to my surprise, we have found out that online video services are a wonderful tool to activate WD-40 Company's "just cause," which is "To make life better at work and at home." We have had, for instance, a lunch-and-learn class where a chef has demonstrated healthy cooking techniques from his kitchen.

And even your average business meetings can take on a flair of their own. I caught wind of how our French team held a business meeting over dinner. But not just any ordinary dinner (but, really, in France, is there ever such a thing?). The members cooked their own dinners in their own kitchens while chatting about business at hand. Then took their plates—and glasses of wine, of course—to their respective dinner tables, and turned the meeting into a virtual—and yet very real—dinner party. (I predict that one of these days, these stories will be told in business schools as a dynamic for highest-level collaborative thinking. Let's give it a name, shall we? How about The Baguette Effect?)

And we are able to include everyone all around the world, all at the same time. A couple of weeks ago we had an all-hands celebration of our 67th birthday. We didn't bring the company to our headquarters—which we affectionately refer to as our tepee, in homage to our tribal culture. We didn't have to. We brought the party to the people, the highlight being a world-class (literally) magician in London who live streamed his performance "all the way from my living room" to living rooms all over the world. Some of our tribe members were having breakfast, some lunch, some wine, and some breakfast that was officially the next day. But they were there … everyone who wanted to come.

Some were able to meet my beautiful wife, Maria, for the first time. And we were able to meet their children, perched on laps, as riveted by the performance as their parents were. And, perhaps even more important, their children were able to meet their parents' colleagues and see what nice people their mommies and daddies work with day in and day out.

I recognize, though, that virtual tribes do have their limitations in terms of keeping the culture alive. Whenever I have the occasion to go to the tepee now, I'm struck by the empty sadness of no people being there. We all need people. And I look forward to the day we can return to a working environment where those who want to—when they want to—can return to the workplace and smile at each other face to face, instead of exclusively monitor camera to monitor camera.

But we're keeping the virtual meeting format as well. Those days are with us forever. It will be a yes/and scenario. There is so much good to take in.

And yet there's the matter of those tribal bonfires where we send our fears and successes up into the starry San Diego night sky. We're still puzzling how we can even approach a virtual version of that. And I'm inclined to believe that it's too sacred a ritual to compromise. We need the experience of each other standing in the bright warm glow of the fire sending our burdens into the dark sky.

While I'm not the clairvoyant our London magician most certainly is, I can predict with some confidence the single word that will be written on most of those pieces of paper. Covid.

It won't be long now.

Chapter 13
It's Time to Think About Re-entry

DO YOU SEE what I'm beginning to see? Depending on where you are on the planet, this particular object might appear close, or still far away. Maybe if you didn't look straight at it, but off to the side a little bit, you'll be able to see the faintest hint of it. If you can't, no worries. You'll be able to see it soon enough.

What the heck am I talking about? The light at the end of the tunnel. It's waaaaaay down there, barely a pinprick. But I can see it. Plain as day. The day when everyone comes back to work. They actually leave their house, wearing shoes that match, car keys in hand, ready to be seen by people other than UberEats and Instacart drivers. People they actually work with. Every day. In real-life person. Can you imagine that?

You're probably having a hard enough time thinking about the ramifications of this change in lifestyle for yourself. But in your role as a leader, you're wise to think about how this shift will impact your people as well. No matter how eagerly they might be clamoring to return to work, to return to "normal," they will also be facing the trauma of yet another major life transformation. They will have to re-engineer, yet again, a whole new set of ways of doing things. Of managing their schedules, the ins and outs of their houses. The ins and outs of their workplaces, greeting familiar faces—but coming to learn new people—and themselves—who have transformed utterly over the last 12 months or more.

Things have changed. Routines have changed. People have changed. Everyone will be finding out soon enough the impacts those transformations will have on your lives and your company's culture. It's easy to not think about it right now, because the challenges aren't in your face yet. And, frankly, it might be too soon to realistically expect conclusions and answers that you can act on.

But the time is just right to start asking yourself—and your people—essential questions that will help get the conversation in motion. So, at the very least, come re-opening day, no one will be caught flat-footed.

Here are some questions that I'm exploring right now, in these early days when the light is still way down there, a pinprick at the end of a tunnel that we expect will stretch at least through the future months:

How Well Have We Walked the Wait?

We all know the expression, "walk the talk." When it comes to creating a values-based company culture, walking the talk is crucial to building up experiences and expectations that help us prove our employee value proposition promise. Walking the talk happens at work. But all during this past year of uncertainty, when *at work* is dining room tables around the world, opportunities to walk the talk might not be so obvious to leaders. And then things begin to slip. Tons of emails get misinterpreted. Feelings get hurt. Impatience flares. Objectives get muddled. And no one has the chance to simply walk down the hall to say, "Hey, I'm sorry. That didn't come out the way I had intended it to."

How well has WD-40 Company walked the wait so far? The results from the most recent mini-survey are encouraging. The response to the sentence, "I'm excited about the company's future," has risen four percentage points from 94% to 98%. So that's extremely encouraging. But, in terms of the supportive tribal culture that we have dedicated ourselves to for decades now, this response warms my heart: "My coach keeps me informed about decisions and the events that affect my job." Where the previous survey reported a respectable 89% positive reaction to that sentence, this current report has shown another four percentage point movement upward to 93%.

"Working at WD-40 Company gives me a sense of personal accomplishment," moved up six points from 85% to 91%.

Does this make me personally proud? Of course! I'm human. So if I appear to be bragging, well, I am. But what is more relevant to the leadership conversation in companies around the world is this: Culture, if you take care of it in a committed and detailed way, is resilient. It can withstand just about anything the external circumstance can throw at it. As long as it's in the protective hands of dedicated stewards and servant leaders—*all* the stewards and servant leaders in a company, not just the CEO.

How Have Our People Changed as a Result of the Traumatic Last Year?

It's not overstating matters to say that last year has been transformatively traumatic for all of us—it's just a matter of the degree. Some of us discovered that maybe we're not so disciplined with using this new time flexibility to learn and grow as we thought we were. (Have you seen the meme where a manager asks a direct report what skills he had acquired during lockdown? He blows into an open tea pot, expertly shooting the tea out of the spout and into a teacup halfway across the table. Now, that's a marketable skill.)

But more seriously, the upending of our daily routines is traumatic. Watching our children's mental health decline out of isolation has made us desperate with anxiety. Losing loved ones to Covid without even being able to say good-bye is unspeakable. How many marriages have broken up? In a happier contrast, how many families have grown (it has, after all, been 12 months)?

All our people were shoved into a hero's journey this past year where they were called upon to stare fear in the face, marshal the extreme frontiers of their own capacity for courage and faith in the unseeable. They're coming back to work different people. Period. How you choose to respond to the answers to this question, is something only you can answer. But honoring and respecting the experiences that all your people have endured in the solitude of their homes—without the support networks and relationships at work and other face-to-face communities—is a great place to start.

What Are Your People Worried About as They Anticipate Returning to Work?

One of my tribe members confided in me the other day that she's worried about leaving her cats alone all day after they've been used to having her around 24/7/365. (A cat expert in my circle reassured me that multiple cat households will be just fine for eight-hour stretches. Dogs, on the other hand, well, that's another matter altogether.) I would venture to say that millions of people around the planet will regret putting off that diet and treadmill routine when they dig out their office clothes for the first time in months. All those freshly vacated homes block after block after block—are they targets for opportunistic criminals?

Last but certainly not least … all those children returning to school … There will be adjustments to be made there. Even though they may have been begging to return to school, even though they once knew the routines of sitting in desks and focusing on the in-person teacher in front of the class, those were long-ago days. A year in a child's life, is, well, a lifetime. And there will be some unexpected twists and turns as children readjust to that daily routine they had longed for for so long.

Will This Period of Re-entry Turn Out to Be a Great Migration Back? Or Will It Become a Great Diaspora?

If your people experience difficulty returning to work, they might conclude that maybe they have outgrown their jobs, or they're no longer enchanted by your company and its mission, or, for any number of reasons, it's time to search for greener pastures. They have, after all, had a lot of time to recon-sider their lives, their choices, and their destinies.

I'm assuming you love your people, and you want what is best for them. If this means that they have wisely concluded that their time to change careers has come, you wish them well. But you also want them to stay for all the right reasons. And how you handle their welcome back will send them the message that a rewarding future is here with you and your company if they want it.

No matter what is on the minds of your cherished tribe members, as they prepare to re-enter the career life they were once used to, and now seems foreign to some degree, they will be coming back to you changed individuals who have been on an amazing adventure of their own.

They will be leaving behind a former version of themselves, and step-ping into a new life. It may look hauntingly familiar. And yet, so different.

While it's still too soon to really know much of anything for sure, there is one thing I do know for sure: It's not too soon to start asking the questions. And ask them again and again as the months unfurl into the future, and then, ideally very soon, as things—hopefully—start getting back to normal.

Whatever that will be.

Epilogue: The Never-Ending Learning Moment

AND SO. HERE we are. At this writing, we're not even halfway through 2021 yet. And the planet is still full of questions about what's in store for us Covid-wise. We have hope. We have metrics. We have protocols. We have vaccinations. We have variants. We have ways to continue to moving forward. We have months marked out on our calendars by which we fully expect to have returned to some kind of normal—it might be a "new normal," but it will be a form of normal just the same. Maybe it will be just another phase, a transition period.

It will be what it will be. That's the one thing we know that we can say for sure. As with just about anything else in life, it's up to us to optimize the good, minimize the bad, and do all this while staying true to our values and commitments to the people in our lives. And we will still make mistakes along the way. Such is the gift of the Learning Moment.

As you have already read several times in this book, the Learning Moment philosophy supports us and keeps us feeling safe as we move into and out of a succession of "fire swamps." We have established what defines Learning Moments: "Positive or negative outcomes from any situation that need to be openly and freely shared to benefit all." And it is my job—indeed it's everyone's job—to use Learning Moments to help us with one of our most essential values: "Make it better than it is today."

Within the WD-40 Company tribe, everyone embraces and benefits from the concept of the Learning Moment equally. Which is fortunate for me because I am most frequently in the position of being able to say "I don't know," and model that level of humble openness to shifting variables in such a way that everyone else can say "I don't know" without fear of embarrassment or reprisal.

This has been especially true over the last accumulating months that are piling up deep into the second year of this experience.

As you may remember from your reading, my motto is *ancora imparo*, which roughly translates into "I am still learning." (It sounds more impressive in the Italian, don't you think? In English, it loses a certain worldly flair.) And I'm still learning from this Unexpected Learning Moment.

(Another one of my favorite expressions is "I'm probably wrong and roughly right." Business leaders throughout the world do themselves an injustice by believing that their power and authority come from a demeanor of unshakeable confidence—even in the face of something as earth-shaking as Covid-19. I, on the other hand, learned years ago that, in the WD-40 Company culture at least, it's not about power and authority to begin with. It's about that tribal culture where the leader is there to serve. And part of being a servant leader is being comfortable enough in our own skin to recognize that we can't possibly know everything. There is bound to be someone inside our tribe who knows more than we do about any given subject. We welcome their knowledge—even corrections. And even being wrong—or at least roughly right—gives us yet another opportunity to show our tribe members that we're all as safe as we can be within our circle of belonging. Will leaders emerge from the Covid-19 nightmare humbled or humiliated? It all depends on how easy they are in time when no one in this world knows anything for sure.)

But there is one thing that I *must* keep top of mind on a daily basis, with so much clarity that my tribe members can count on my allegiance to the vision:

No matter what comes our way—unexpected Learning Moments, both good and bad—my duty to everyone inside the WD-40 Company tribe, including our customers, is to support them in creating positive, lasting memories that they will be able to pass on to generations: "This is how we created a culture of safety and belonging at a time when the only thing we knew for absolute certain was the fact that we could count on each other."

And we thrived.

About Garry Ridge

As chairman and chief executive officer of WD-40 Company, Garry Ridge is responsible for developing and implementing high-level strategies, all operations, and the oversight of all relationships and partnerships for the company.

Garry is passionate about the learning and empowering organizational culture he has helped establish at the WD-40 Company, and his vision and leadership have positively impacted the WD-40 Company in both measurable and immeasurable ways. Garry joined WD-40 Company in 1987 and has held various management positions in the company, including executive vice president and chief operating officer, and vice president of international. He has worked directly with WD-40 Company in over 70 countries.

Garry is an adjunct professor at the University of San Diego where he teaches the principles and practices of corporate culture in the Master of Science in Executive Leadership program. In 2009, he co-authored a book with Ken Blanchard outlining his effective leadership techniques, entitled *Helping People Win at Work: A Business Philosophy called "Don't Mark My Paper, Help Me Get an A"* (Pearson, 2009). More recently, he was a contributor to the book *Work is Love Made Visible: Finding Your Purpose From the World's Greatest Thought Leaders*, edited by Marshall Goldsmith, Frances Hesselbein, and Sarah MacArthur (Wiley, 2018). He also contributed a chapter to the book, *The Freedom of Constraints: Turn Obstacles Into Opportunity*, edited by Darcy Verhun.

A native of Australia, Garry holds a certificate in Modern Retailing and Wholesale Distribution and a Master of Science in Executive Leadership from the University of San Diego. He has also been named one of the Top 10 Most Admired CEOs in the World by Inc. Magazine. And in 2021 Global Gurus ranked him at #9 in its list of top 30 leadership experts in the world.

To learn more, visit www.thelearningmoment.net

About Martha I. Finney

Martha I. Finney is the author or co-author of 27 books on HR, leadership, employee engagement, and career management. Her bestsellers include *HR From the Heart: Inspiring Stories and Strategies for Building the People Side of Great Business*, which she wrote with Libby Sartain, former CHRO of Southwest Airlines and Yahoo.

Her most recent book is *Healing at Work: A Guide to Using Career Conflicts to Overcome Your Past and Build the Future You Deserve*, with Susan Schmitt Winchester, CHRO of Applied Materials.

She is also a publishing and platform consultant and coach, helping an exclusive clientele expand their professional thought leadership brand by leveraging publishing and social media. Her clients and interviewees come from such companies as Intuit, GM, JetBlue, Avery Dennison, Starwood Hotels and Resorts, Marriott, Caterpillar, Sears Holdings, Patagonia, the U.S. Marine Corps, HP, and SAS Institute.

Her own original research into employee engagement has been featured in *The Wall Street Journal*, *The New York Times*, *The Washington Post*, *Miami Herald*, *The San Francisco Chronicle*, *The San Jose Mercury News*, *Time* Magazine, The Huffington Post, CNN, NPR, among other business media outlets.

To learn more, visit www.marthafinney.global

Made in the USA
Columbia, SC
09 June 2021